SOROR
MYSTICA

AN ALCHEMICAL OPUS

MATHEW MATHER

SOROR MYSTICA

AN ALCHEMICAL OPUS

MATHEW MATHER

Soror Mystica: An Alchemical Opus
Copyright 2025 Mathew Mather

ISBN (hardcover) : 978-1-917898-06-5
ISBN (paperback): 978-1-917898-07-2
ISBN (EPUB): 978-1-917898-08-9

First printed December, 2025
by Sul Books (an imprint of Sul Books, LTD)
Lewes, UK / Rodenbourg, LUX
Cover and Interior Design: Sul Books

Find our other titles at SULBOOKS.COM

The art is queen of the alchemist's heart, she is at once his mother, his daughter, and his beloved, and in his art and its allegories the drama of his own soul, his individuation process, is played out.[1]

---

[1] C. G. Jung, "Mysterium Coniunctionis" (1955/1956), in *CW*, vol. 14 (London: Routledge & Kegan Paul, 1981), par. 543.

CONTENTS

ACKNOWLEDGEMENTS

First and foremost, I would like to thank the women in my life. Special mentions to my mother, Maeve, my wife, Lyn, and my two lovely daughters, Katie and Karla. My sister Alice, and niece Karen. Also, Jude Passia (a layer in my psyche) and Katherine. You have all been a continued source of love, joy, and inspiration.

I would also like to thank my brother Dinty and my nephews Nic and Jack. Each of you is a *Frater Mysticus* to me, with an intuitive grasp and appreciation of my arcane interests. In hopes that our paths join up more often, despite being on different continents. Also, I would like to thank my good Clonmel friend Dr Sean Moran, Street Philosopher, who passed away a couple of years ago. Our friendship appears on occasion in this work.

Much gratitude and appreciation to our students on the *Certificate in Jungian Psychology with Art Therapy* over the past 14 years, our students on the *MA in Art, Psyche and the Creative Imagination*, over the past few years, and my PhD students as part of our Art and Psyche research group. Special mentions to my first PhD graduates, Dr. Lisa Hester (Re-Envisioning Visionary Art) and Dr. Teresa Mason (Sheela-na-gig), who both excelled with much dedication. It was a pleasure and an honour to be part of your projects. Special gratitude and appreciation also for our local and international faculty who have generously added their unique "touch of magic" into the vessel of our work. A special mention to Robert Romanyshyn, whose amazing inspiration and insight has been core to our adventure. All of our work together has been and continues to be, in so many ways, *the true story of an alchemical opus*.

Many thanks to our dear friends. I will not mention names, but you know who you are.

Special thanks to my editor, Rhyd Wildermuth, for his time and valuable insight to help shape this work. I especially appreciate his encouragement of the various uncanny, anomalous, exceptional, and synchronistic experiences that characterise much of this work.

$$\approx$$

A special note is that I have, in the main, avoided the use of names. This said, I have on occasion included personalities. Where this is fairly substantial, I have requested, and been granted, their permission. For this I give heartfelt thanks.

PROLOGUE

A Scallop Shell; Three (+) Kinds of Love; Anima Mundi; Alchemy; Astrology; Tarot

This alchemical adventure began in my adolescent years. It was ignited by an astrological prediction, a secret love, enigmatic dreams, and, of course, a psychopomp in the guise of Swiss psychologist Carl Gustav Jung. I could not know, back in the heady days of my youth, where this would all end up. My life, ordinary in most ways, would become one of soul-making in a largely soulless world.

There is an excerpt from Jack Haas' book *In, and Of: Memoirs of a Mystic Journey Along Canada's Wild West Coast* that I share with our students each year for my day on Alchemy:

> The *soror mystica*, or, mystical sister, is the female half of the male-female partnership. In alchemical lore these two work together seeking the philosopher's stone, or Holy Grail.
>
> My *soror* and I were brought together by the invisible choreographer, as the saying goes, through a series of dreams and unexpected happenings, which also will be related later. She quickly became my lover, consort, and colleague, as we entered upon the same path, towards a destination neither of us could have imagined.
>
> The alchemical partnership seeks, in essence, to find each person's own divinity through the conscious assistance of another who, in intimate relationship, mirrors back all the aspects of the other's soul which lay hidden; aspects which either taint or cloud the polished vision through which God could otherwise see clearly through human eyes. It is a lengthy process, one requiring commitment and humility to allow its rare completion. But, in fact, every coupleship or marriage is itself the crucible in which this process takes place, albeit mostly on a dark and unconscious level, and therefore everywhere on earth there is the possibility of husband and wife learning about themselves- via the other's stimulation — and of all that lays hidden within, including each one's dormant alter-gender other half; i.e. the man's female side, and the female's male side. And in doing so each reaches a wholeness

in which the spirit comes to inhabit the flesh, the two become one, and heaven and earth are united through them.[2]

A Scallop Shell

In writing this, I recall a recent memory from a trip west to the Dingle peninsula in Ireland. This was part of a surprise trip for my 60th birthday, organised by my wife and our two daughters. We have nostalgic memories of regular summer holidays here, during the years of our daughters' childhood.

The recollection of this most recent trip was of a morning walk along Ventry beach, a few miles outside the seaside village of Dingle. During much of the walk, Lyn and I were separate, doing beachy things at our own pace. Towards the end of our walk, meeting up again, I had a little gift for her: a scallop shell. Her nickname as a child was Shelly. The scallop shell, in particular, was the association. This particular shell I have come to know as the pilgrim shell, pointing the way for travellers along the now-famed Camino de Santiago in Spain.

During one of my walks on this very beach some summers ago, I found three scallop shells. Different in size, they neatly fitted into each other like Russian dolls, and each shell was of a different colour: black, red, and white. In alchemy, the three important colour changes, symbolic of the soul's transformational journey, transition from black (*nigredo*) to white (*albedo*) to red (*rubedo*). So, these three shells came to symbolise for me an alchemical journey that has largely characterised our lives together.

Back to the Ventry beach walk. I gave the scallop shell to Lyn, and it turned out that she, too, had a gift for me — also a scallop shell. My shell was flat with one side a creamy white, and the other an orangey-brown. Hers was more curved and creamy white on both sides. This was the only time, in our twenty-five years of marriage, that we exchanged a scallop shell gift. Walking along the beach together, I held both of them in my hands and noticed that they were actually the

---

[2] Haas, Jack. *In, and Of: Memoirs of a Mystic Journey Along Canada's Wild West Coast.* (Iconoclast Press, 2002), 13.

same size, within a millimetre or so. This was quite remarkable, a "snap" moment. Two parts of a single being?

A bit later that day, whilst driving in the beautiful Dingle area, it occurred to me that ancient Chinese society was largely oriented around a more holistic and synchronistic worldview. The tortoise was the oracular microcosm, its flat base plate symbolising Earth and the upper curved shell as Heaven. A divinatory system had been devised using the tortoise shell, informing decision-making for the state. Later, this would evolve into the more familiar *I Ching*, the *Book of Changes*. This all reminded me of the upper and lower scallop shells from our beach walk. Some of our work together, following especially the pioneering work of Carl Jung, revolves around a playful exploration of such an alternative worldview. Such a perspective is largely anathema to the mainstream zeitgeist of contemporary Western culture.

I reflected on our lives and work together. We had both shape-shifted a few years hence from careers that were long past "due by" dates; Lyn's in housing and architecture, mine in sustainable energy and technology. After being made redundant, Lyn embarked on retraining as an Art Therapist. I began a part time PhD on Jung and alchemy. We followed a dream and a calling. Combining our skills we formed a part-time course: "Certificate in Jungian Psychology with Art Therapy" with the support of local Irish Jungians.[3] As a follow-on, we also conceived an MA in Art, Psyche and the Creative Imagination.[4] This work constitutes much of our "alchemical opus." Accordingly, what follows includes a weave of stories and experiences associated with this work. It is our labour of love.

_____

[3] In September 2023 we enter the 14th year of its running.

[4] This year, 2023, sees our first cohort of graduates from this three-year part-time programme.

THREE (+) KINDS OF LOVE

Upon further contemplation of our two halves of the scallop shell, I wondered if they could be from the same organism. Upon closer inspection, the edge serrations do not perfectly align. The two halves are from separate creatures. This observation prompts the old question of whether we have a literal soulmate in the world, or whether we should read it as a metaphor for gendered internal aspects within our psyche. This latter idea chimes with Jung's *anima-animus* notion, whereby our largely unconscious contra-sexual counterpart is autonomously projected onto a significant other. This projection can result, over time and along the precarious path of life, in successive disillusionments. For the ancient Greek Odysseus, this has been interpreted as the various enchantresses along his journey that would eventually lead from problematic encounters with women (such as the Sirens and the sorceress Circe) to an eventual reconnection with his wife, Penelope, as a flesh-and-blood human.

Here, however, I do not wish to embark on an academic discourse on romantic love. My purposes are rather that of memoir, informed by a playful sandpit exploration of the arcane released from academic straightjackets. In this endeavour, and at risk of being labelled out of touch with contemporary gender concerns, I take my lead especially from the feminine. There is a quintessence feminine wherein I discover a life energy, and this is not only sexual.

A *Street Philosopher* column by my late friend, Dr. Sean Moran, has been most helpful in this regard.[5] He touches on a number of kinds of love but gives special attention to three from classical Greek philosophy: *eros*, *philia*, and *agape*.

> The first type, *eros*, is sexually-charged love. Partners may be drawn together romantically by *eros*. The second type of love, *philia*, has no sexual element, and corresponds approximately to 'fondness.' Our family and friends are joined to us by bonds of *philia* (if we're lucky). The third type, *agape* (pronounced 'ah-gah-pay'),

[5] Sean Moran, "Smooching by the Seine," *Philosophy Now*, no. 148 (February/March 2022): 60.

can be defined as 'love for humanity.' The key idea is that *agape* is undeserved or unconditional love. It is a concept from theology. God's love for us is unmerited, since we are all sinners. The implication is that we should in turn love our fellow human beings, whether or not they deserve it. These three concepts aren't always as clear-cut as I have indicated, and I've left out some others, such as *ludus* — playful, flirtatious love.

Nevertheless, *eros*, *philia* and *agape* together form a convenient way of analysing love. There are also good reasons why the lines between these three types should not be blurred, since *eros* can spoil the innocence of other types of love. When *eros* overpowers the brotherly love of *philia*, incest may shrink the gene pool in potentially harmful ways. Or when *eros* outsmarts *agape* in education, professors abuse their power by tinkering with their students' affections, and there is always the suspicion that the relationship is exploitative or transactional (good grades in exchange for services rendered).

The scope of *philia* extends beyond human relationships to encompass wider types of fondness. The word '*philo-sophia*' is of course Greek for 'love of wisdom'. A fondness for the living world is called 'biophilia'. Such love can be taken too far, and become an eroticised zoophilia.

Needless to say, there is also *sisterly love* and *brotherly love*. I have my mystical sisters and mystical brothers: *Sorores Mysticae* and *Fratres Mystici*.

ANIMA MUNDI

There is also another kind of love that relates the part, as our psyche, to a greater whole. In Jung's words:

> The development of Western philosophy during the last two centuries has succeeded in isolating the mind in its own sphere and in severing it from its primordial oneness with the universe. Man himself has ceased to be the microcosm and eidolon of the cosmos, and his 'anima' is no longer the consubstantial scintilla, or spark of the *Anima Mundi*, the World Soul.[6]

Romantic love, for me, intimates connection to a majestic whole. Mythic images such as the *Anima Mundi* remind us of a

---

[6] C. G. Jung, "Psychological Commentary on 'The Tibetan Book of the Great Liberation'" (1954) in *CW*, vol. 8 (London: Routledge & Kegan 1981), par. 759.

sublime beauty and mystery. Viewed in this way, the alchemical opus might be considered a re-connection and communing of individual psyche with *Anima Mundi*. In better appreciating and understanding the symbolic language of psyche, expressed through phenomena such as dreams and synchronicities, we might begin to discover a nostalgia beyond just a temporal life: the homecoming of our soul.

Here we are assuming an en-souled world, as opposed to a largely dead and inert world as espoused by most of contemporary science. Richard Tarnas, in his book *Cosmos and Psyche: Intimations of a New World View* (2008), suggests we imagine "not the disenchanted mechanistic universe of conventional modern cosmology, but rather a deep-souled, subtly mysterious cosmos of great spiritual beauty and creative intelligence" and that this universe "seeks to know you … to unite with you and thereby bring forth something new, a creative synthesis emerging from both of your depths … an intellectual fulfilment that is intimately linked with imaginative vision, moral transformation, empathic understanding, aesthetic delight … an act of love and intelligence combined, of wonder as well as discernment, of opening to a process of mutual discovery."[7] He writes further:

> I believe that the disenchantment of the modern universe is the direct result of a simplistic epistemology and moral posture spectacularly inadequate to the depths, complexity, and grandeur of the cosmos. To assume *a priori* that the entire universe is ultimately a soulless void within which our multidimensional consciousness is an anomalous accident, and that purpose, meaning, conscious intelligence, moral aspiration, and spiritual depth are solely attributes of the human being, reflects a long invisible inflation on the part of the modern self. And heroic hubris is still indissolubly linked, as it was in ancient Greek tragedy, to heroic fall.[8]

We are intrigued by the possibility of discovering intelligent life somewhere in the universe. Our hopes have resulted in costly technologies listening for codes and signals emanat-

---

[7] Richard Tarnas, *Cosmos and Psyche: Intimations of a New World View* (New York, Plume, 2007), 39.

[8] Ibid., 40.

ing from deep space. Yet there is a profound wisdom and intelligence closer to home in our psyche and in the psyche of the world. Surely it is our task in the 21ˢᵗ century to restore this relationship. Jung's *symbolic life* provides a key to access this "treasure in the field," for aligning inner and outer, of being in Tao, and of living in a state of grace.

ALCHEMY

An important alchemical image is in a 16ᵗʰ-century alchemical treatise, the *Rosarium Philosophorum* (Rosary of the Philosophers).[9] Of the different versions of the *Rosarium Philosophorum*, the one I prefer aesthetically is done using colour line drawings by the Czech alchemist Jaroš Griemiller, dated 1578.[10]

This image depicts a naked King-Sun and Queen-Moon. Their hands form a circuit through the medium of two roses. The King's right hand holds the rose stem, with the flower in the Queen's left hand. The Queen's left hand holds the rose stem, with the flower in the King's right hand. Above, and descending between them, is a dove of the Holy Spirit and/or the bird of Hermes. They are enclosed in a mandorla-shaped Latin script.

The *Rosarium* offers a series of images that can be interpreted as transformations in an alchemical *vas* (vessel), such as the process of uniting gold with silver by means of a purification and then a melting down within a solvent, such as mercury, to create a unified and magical substance. In the Renaissance alchemical imagination, the worldview was holistic. Processes in the *vas*, for instance, would have synchronistic correspondences between alchemist and *soror mystica*, reflections of their inner as well as the outer world. In this worldview, a system of correspondences (poetic affinities) implies resonances of like-with-like. For instance, we get

---

[9] The meaning is apparently related to a "rose garden" and not the familiar Catholic rosary.

[10] Jung chose a different version, as a woodcut series dated 1550, for his book *Psychology of the Transference*.

a chain of correspondences such as Sun — King — Gold; and Moon — Queen — Silver. The alchemical transformation in the *vas* coincides meaningfully with psychospiritual transformations of alchemist and *soror mystica*.

In the sequence, the alchemist and *soror mystica* undergo a number of radical transformations. In the woodcut version, they end up in a mercurial *vas*. This progresses to them being submerged in an erotic embrace, followed by the emergence of wings. They then become fused in a rectangular tomb. A few stages later, a single resurrected winged and androgynous being emerges. It is unclear whether the sequence refers to processes going on within the *vas*, or whether it depicts the alchemical couple. This ambiguity could have been intentional, highlighting the *participation mystique* of the couple with the transformation of substances.

For Jung, the sequence usefully portrays psychological states along the path of individuation that takes place between analyst and analysand, culminating in an integrated wholeness. In his psychology, simply put, the individual undergoes a deconstruction (*dissolutio*), death (*mortificatio*), and rebirth (*renovatio*). The process thus mirrors a quintessential symbol of the mystery of transformation (butterfly, scarab, moth), from worm to pupa to winged being. In this regard, one might also consider the Sufi scholar Henry Corbin's understanding of "becoming an angel" (Angelomorphism). The erotic undertones of this particular sequence also suggest the vital role of (sexual) libido.[11]

The alchemical image on the cover of this book is from the 17th-century *Mutus Liber*. Here, once again, we see alchemist, *soror mystica*, and the *vas*. Their earthly *opus*, or labour, that takes place below has a correspondence with angelic beings in a heavenly realm above. The realms are separated, yet we see a foot from each angel penetrating through to the earthly human world. This suggests that the work of the alchemist and the *soror mystica* is correlated to a celestial and eternal

---

[11] With recent scientific developments there is scope for researching the relationship between alchemy (as Jung understood it) and developmental neuropsychology.

realm, emphasising the *As Above, So Below* maxim of the Hermetic mystery. Furthermore, in this alchemical sequence, the couple is mostly clothed, perhaps symbolic of an alternative (platonic) path in which libido becomes sublimated into the work.

Over the past decade and a half, Lyn and I, as a couple that co-created a way of teaching Jungian and Depth Psychology, have witnessed numerous students journeying through the courses we offer. The combination of experiential-based Art with Jungian, post-Jungian and Depth Psychology, and locating personal process as a foundation stone for the work, has proven most fascinating and often transformational.

ASTROLOGY

My interest in Jung came through astrology. It all began in my early teens with an astrological prediction, a secret love, and big dreams. The story goes that my mother and her friend went to consult an astrologer living in a caravan in Cape Town when I must have been about twelve or thirteen years old. She was aghast as the astrologer had correctly predicted the subsequent break-up of her (seemingly) stable marriage. She was so impressed, though, that she decided to embark on a study of this ancient art.

The astrologer also predicted I would fall deeply in love with someone whose Moon was in Scorpio, and that I would marry and leave home. Having my Moon in Sagittarius, he likened this relationship to the mythic St. George (Sagittarius) and the Dragon (Scorpio); intensely attracted yet locked in mortal combat.

Of course, not surprisingly for a fifteen-year-old, I did fall very much in love. However, contrary to the prediction, I did not leave home or get married. The uncanny thing is that my beloved then had a Moon in Scorpio in her astrological chart. This accuracy was intriguing and initiated me into a more serious study of astrology.

By seventeen years of age, I had learnt enough to set up as an astrologer. In this self-education, the occasional reference to Jung was especially fascinating. By this stage, I was also undergoing two years of military conscription and ended up as a dog handler in the South African Air Force. It was during this time that I awoke one morning to an enigmatic dream. In the dream, a voice proclaimed: "God is symbolized by a white Sagittarian Dragon." Such a mysterious association that identified the divinity, my love, and me was fascinating. Subsequently, with the help especially of Jung's alchemical works and astrology, I began to unravel an uncanny sophistication to this relatively simple dream fragment. What was especially intriguing was how the dream conflated a secret love to the divine.

In astrology, the Moon is associated to the occult, the nocturnal, and the unconscious side of the psyche. A Lunar relationship, as *hidden love,* suggests the subterranean and the esoteric as opposed to a relationship defined by the bright light of Solar consciousness. Scorpio and Sagittarius also form an interesting pair: they combine a number of opposing qualities. Scorpio is a fixed water and feminine sign, whereas Sagittarius is a mutable fire and masculine sign. Images associated to Scorpio include the eagle, snake, dragon, and scorpion, whereas the dominant image of Sagittarius is the Centaur (horse from the waist down and human from the waist up). As a relationship, there is a richness of binary oppositions: fire/water, mutable/fixed, male/female, and animal/human in a tension that finds a compelling amplification in the legend of St George and the Dragon.

Some months later, whilst on leave from the Air Force and visiting a friend in Johannesburg, I bought Jung's autobiography, *Memories, Dreams, Reflections.* On the train back to my hometown of Kimberley, having recently completed reading this book, I had another unusual experience in the early evening. Lying in bed, I was lulled into a pleasant sleep state by the rhythmic clicking and gentle rocking of the train. In what I presume must have been a hypnagogic state, I had a vision of myself eating hot coals. After eating my fill, my stomach glowed with the fiery heat. A few moments later, my entire being transformed through my solar plexus into a black and fiery Sagittarian Dragon. In a state of shock, I jolted back into waking consciousness.

The basic meaning was immediately apparent. Eating hot coals was symbolic of consuming the content of *Memories, Dreams, Reflections*. The emphasis here was on the powerful, transformative, and dark energy of the God-image which Jung's work made so clear, in contrast to the more serene white Sagittarian Dragon. The train was also powered by hot coals. There was a resonance of being powered psychically by intense and compact energy. A further detail was the direction of the train from Johannesburg (renowned for its gold) to Kimberley (renowned for its diamonds). This hinted at the journey of life in terms of an alchemical transformation and at the great value to be discovered in the subterranean ground of the unconscious.

By this stage, I was so struck by Jung that I resolved to sell the few worldly assets I had to purchase his *Collected Works*. Soon after military service, at the tender age of twenty, this aspiration was realised. Amidst my university studies of psychology and anthropology, I immersed myself in these arcane works. It was especially his later works, on alchemy, that shed further light on my dream. A few excerpts from *The Spirit Mercurius* from the *Collected Works, Volume 13*, are illustrative.

> Because of his united double nature Mercurius is described as hermaphroditic. Sometimes his body is said to be masculine and his soul feminine, sometimes the reverse ... He is also called husband and wife, bridegroom and bride, or loved and beloved...and in Khunrath he is 'begotten of the hermaphroditic seed of the Macrocosm' as 'an immaculate birth from the hermaphroditic matter.'[12]

> Water and fire are classic opposites and can be valid definitions of one and the same thing only if this thing unites in itself the contrary qualities of water and fire. The psychologem 'Mercurius' must therefore possess an essentially antinomial dual nature.[13]

---

[12] C. G. Jung, "The Spirit Mercurius" (1942/1953), in *CW*, vol. 13 (London: Routledge & Kegan Paul, 1981), par. 268.

[13] Ibid., 266.

Mercurius represents the 'continuous cohabitation' which is found in unalloyed form in the Tantric Shiva-Shakti concept.[14]

The two substances of Mercurius are thought of as dissimilar, sometimes opposed; as the dragon he is 'winged and wingless.'[15]

Here, we see in the abstruse alchemical imagination an uncanny semblance of the above amplifications with the heart of my dream image. Mercurius as two lovers — yet mysteriously one — in a state of continuous cohabitation: divine and cosmic, yet fickle and earthly, a union of fire and water, and as two dragons of contrary natures. Such images further evoked the numinosity of my love affair as a mystical wedding or *heiros gamos*; the paradisiacal feeling of the Self as a love relationship. In effect, the *coniunctio* (conjunction, or union) also takes place in the *vas* of the psyche.

The experience as a whole — of the love affair, the dreams and images, and of my search into their meaning — sparked what may be described as a mystical pilgrimage and as a journey of renewal. What was previously a chimera of ideas borrowed from a range of esoteric sources was satisfyingly integrated in the comprehensive wholeness of alchemy as depicted by Jung. The strange ideas of God in nature, God in me, God existing in Heaven and Hell, God as a mystical love affair and as a mysterious union of opposites, God as libidinous passion, both erotic and spiritual, and of God in a state of becoming and of humanity's purpose in this, are all integral to such a view.

As I later realised, this dream also corresponded in an essential way to the notion of the alchemical *coniunctio* (associated with the dawning of a new astrological Age, as Aquarius), after the previous Christian Age that was characterised by a *separatio*. Here, a spontaneous manifestation from the unconscious would appear to have corroborated one of Jung's central notions.

Many years later, during my PhD research, I would assemble a life myth construction of Jung by weaving three threads

---

[14] Ibid., 278.

[15] Ibid., 267.

derived from his alchemical worldview, his belief in the transition of the Ages from Pisces to Aquarius, and the Grail Legend.[16]

Tarot

My mother not only introduced me to astrology but also to the Tarot. In times of financial difficulties, after an acrimonious divorce, she would occasionally do card readings. When I was about twelve or thirteen years old, she gave me a pack, the Rider-Waite Tarot, snugly housed in a silken bag with Chinese-like letterings on its cover spelling my initials. I still have these cards.

I also did card readings, though I never felt a convincing sense of mastery. Over the years, they remained a mere side act, compared to a more vibrant interest in astrology.

For a number of years, Lyn and I would sometimes do a short Tarot spread when gathered with friends for the New Year, comprised of five cards in a cross formation and another four cards as the elaboration of the theme. To be honest, I would often scratch my head at the value of this exercise. Even these few cards challenged my interpretive powers, often leading to bafflement. I had also not undergone any extensive study of the practice, and so my knowledge was rather threadbare, limited to Jungian-style associations and amplifications of the symbolism. This interest began to fade.

On the 31st of December 2015, we attended a New Year's Eve party. I had mixed feelings this year about even bringing the cards to the celebration. They ended up staying in the bag, untouched. The following morning, the 1st of January 2016, in the kitchen of our stone cottage in the Nire valley, I was the first one up. Over a coffee and light breakfast, I stared at the pack of cards on the table. A curious impulse took over, and I found myself spreading them out in the usual face down. I then decided to draw a single card.

---

[16] I later reformulated this into a book publication *The Alchemical Mercurius: Esoteric Symbol of Jung's Life and Works* (Routledge 2013).

Turning my selected card face up, I was unnerved to discover it was card XIII, Death. The hairs on the back of my head felt as if they literally stood up. Out of the seventy-eight cards, this is the one that was selected! This was not a comforting divinatory message, considering the circumstances of our lives at the time.

❧

The book focuses on a selection of narratives that span eight years of my life from 2016 up to the end of 2023. On, or near, the 1st of January for each of these years I (we) did a divinatory draw of a Tarot card from the major arcana. The card selected formed a symbol to contemplate over the course of the year. Notable experiences such as encounters, dreams and synchronistic phenomena were subsequently journaled. These comprised a *prima materia* that was then mined, worked upon, and rendered into this work, an alchemical Opus. Each chapter/year/card consists of a few personal stories. Together they form a mosaic that coheres around the symbolism of the years Tarot card. Stylistically each story typically includes journal excerpts interleaved with a story line and commentary.

2016: DEATH (XIII)

Irish Economic Collapse; In the Hands of the Gods; Saint Patrick's Cemetery; Fish Poisoning; Death of a Friend; Herbie; A Brush with Death

In the Rider-Waite Tarot, the Death card shows a Black Knight riding a white Horse. On the ground is a dead King with two children grieving on their knees. Beside them is a Bishop in a rite of death. To the right, in the distance and across a river, are two towers of a medieval city entrance, with a Sun either rising or setting between them. A sailboat is in the river, with the wind taking it to the right.

The Marseille deck is simpler. It depicts the Grim Reaper as a skeleton with a blood-red scythe. Two dismembered bodies litter the ground, including a crowned head in the lower right (King) and a female head at the lower left.

The symbolism in the card is of an outworn modality (hero, King) being dismembered and of Death as a precursor toward renewal. The ambiguity of the Sun (as either setting or rising) portrays both death (setting) and resurrection (rising). The Marseilles card indicates this as fresh shoots appearing from the ground, pointing to the cyclical round of nature. In alchemy, this card corresponds to *mortificatio* as precursor to the *nigredo*, the dark night of the soul.

The skeletal bones suggest a deepening awareness of an essence that outlives the transitory flesh and blood. Bones as a *memento mori* remind us of our own mortality, of our ancestral kinship, and of the eternal soul. They recall a deep wisdom, as a "feeling in our bones." This card can coincide with a life crisis that can ultimately bring us back to the essentials in our lives. It may allow for an opportunity to reorient via a reconnection with the compass of our soul.

In one commentary, we read:

> Traditional in the initiation of a knight was the final confrontation with the mysterious Black Knight, an unknown warrior armed with a primitive axe, who demanded that the initiate lay his neck on the block. If the young man had the courage to obey this fateful command, the mysterious stranger threw down his

axe and lifted his visor, revealing himself as a saviour of shining countenance.[17]

IRISH ECONOMIC COLLAPSE

Tarot card commentaries optimistically tend to emphasise the symbolic nature of the card: that it refers to a death *in this life*, regeneration, and renewal. However, it didn't feel this way for me. As a family, we were dealt a convergence of challenges in the past years, starting with the spectacular recession in Ireland in 2008. From two professional salaries, we were down to one, as Lyn's contract in architecture and planning was discontinued as a result of the recession. With each new budget, my salary took successive cuts. Our variable-interest mortgage rate kept climbing. We did not have the resources to modernise our stone cottage in the Nire valley. We were (and still are) a one-car family and had to dispense with health insurance. I did a foolish thing by taking out loans to service an ever-increasing mortgage, fearful of falling into arrears. The words "insufficient funds" at the ATM nearing month's end became a regular stress.

Our lives had been in economic free-fall for a number of years. We were in debt, with negative equity, and in big trouble. We still had daily half-hour commutes from the valley to school and work with no public transport. Typically, on a couple of the weekdays, I'd need to lecture early on another campus in Thurles. This entailed an extra forty minutes' commute. I have memories of having to drop our daughters off on some cold and rainy winter mornings at McDonald's (the only place open at the time), with instructions to walk to school from there.

I wondered at our situation, having dedicated many years to education and a professional career, for us to end up like this! I shuddered to think how the country's bankruptcy impacted so many of the families in Ireland. We were certainly no isolated case and by far not the worst. This was a time

---

[17] Sallie Nichols, *Jung and Tarot: An Archetypal Journey* (New York: Weiser Books, 1980/1998), 233.

when the number of suicides reported, especially in males, increased significantly. The stress of it all had also impacted my health in subtle ways. A malaise had settled in.

A repeating image often plagued me: the sound of the Titanic having hit an iceberg, cold, eerie, and full of dark foreboding. Our daughters were on a mantra that we should move to town. Lyn had joined in, yet I couldn't see the way forward with such a plan financially. It would mean a decisive rupture with our current precarious situation and would deepen our problems.

As a family, we watched the DVD *No Escape* (2015), featuring Owen Wilson and Pierce Brosnan, around Christmas of that year. The story is of a family — a mother, father, and two young daughters (Owen Wilson acting as the father) — arriving in a foreign Asian country for career purposes. On the day of their arrival, a political coup grips the country, with violence breaking out in the streets, including their hotel. At one point in the drama, they are stuck on top of a building with insurgents on the chase. Their only escape is to jump onto the roof of a nearby building. This appears impossible for any adult, let alone the young daughters. The cinematography and emotion-building established a perilous, vertiginous crossing for the family. Miraculously, however, they managed to get across. After a harrowing ordeal, including becoming separated from each other, they end up reunited as a family and return to safety.

Themes from this film would recur during 2016, as it seemed to have parallels with the debacle we faced. Pulling the Death card on New Year's Day did not seem to bode well. With symbolic knowledge, though, I held optimistically to the hope of rebirth after a symbolic death. During the year, we would still be entangled in visits to various financial advisors. My career was also in transition, being caught in-between the old as a career in technology and the new as a redeployment in the arts faculty. During the first semester of 2016, with advice from my union, I held onto an unrealistic workload split between the two faculties. The old had not yet died, and the new had not yet been born. Like a snake casting off an old skin, I wondered at times whether I would make it through this precarious transition. Meanwhile, our creation of the Certificate in Jungian Psychology with Art Therapy — started in 2009 — had helped us to navigate the choppy recessional waters. This was a godsend, giving that extra bit of finance.

IN THE HANDS OF THE GODS

Some months into the year, having finally decided to let our house go, we moved from the Nire Valley to our market town of Clonmel. Thanks to our daughters' connections, we managed to secure a nice, suburban home to rent. This physical move was a dangerous crossing, as we didn't have the finances to do this. I had no option but to max out our credit cards, knowing full well there was no hope of realistically repaying any of it. I took out successive cash withdrawals over a two- or three-day period. At this point, the image of that dangerous jump in the *No Escape* film had proved itself to be most prescient.

During this time, I had also developed an incessant cough and was generally feeling out of sorts. Our literal move into town in the autumn occurred on the 15th of October, 2016, coinciding with a super, Hunter's, Full Moon (Libra-Aries).[18] The first day of our arrival, we were met with a rainbow clearly visible from our front door, seemingly stretching from the side of the river Suir we used to live (in County Waterford) to the Tipperary side. I cherished the moment, insisting on taking a couple of photos of Lyn in the foreground. This was a welcome and beautiful omen for our new life and safe crossing, as if divine grace was behind the significant life change. It felt as if our lives were in "the hands of the gods," and that we were living in a state of grace. That first evening, our friends insisted on bringing a venison stew. It fitted the moment as a *Hunter's* Full Moon.

---

[18] We had moved into our Nire valley home during a solar eclipse in Gemini some years back (31st of May 2003).

We moved into town from the Nire Valley just over 2 weeks ago. The word 'spaciousness' explains a lot about the change. Living in the valley for the past 12 or 13 years leaves so much to reflect on, such as the first few golden years (in many ways) of our daughters enjoying the garden and country life. It was the Celtic Tiger with freedom to explore, to do things and to buy things. The last few years though — we suffered cold, damp, and mould. Spider webs everywhere, things were breaking down and we had no money to fix anything. Windows broken, roof tiles dislodging, wood pellet heater broken. Financial pressures to the point of our whole life eventually 'imploding' — eventually resulting in our only option being to move on.

Fortunately, though, the Cosmos is surely smiling on us as, for now, we have a soft landing. We are now living in a spacious, modern house, in a 'leafy' estate within walking distance from town.

A scene from the alchemical Splendor Solis *comes to mind — of the Sun, amidst a fairly devastated landscape. Despite the devastation, there is a sense of spiritual autumn – of death, but also something soulful at the closing of a 'day' yet perhaps the sunrise of a 'new day'.*

Driving to work a few days before leaving the valley – in the autumn morning — crossing the Suir bridge — the sunlight and autumn colours on the river. A quiet splendour. A quiet satisfaction. An acceptance of my life and circumstances despite much loss. We still have many blessings, for which I am so very grateful for. My healthy, lovely daughters.

Yesterday evening I found a St Patrick's pendant in my cupboard, with a St Nicholas on the other side.

I had a dream that my mother had fixed our house in the valley. In a way, this dream has come true, in that now we are in a repaired house.

SAINT PATRICK'S CEMETERY

Our new home is in an estate off Saint Patrick's Road, next to the town cemetery. A regular walk would now require going through the cemetery, across a main road and into a lovely park that leads onto the Suir river.

This walk, cutting through the cemetery, would induce frequent contemplations on death and of a *memento mori* ("remember we must die"). We would be witnessing the cemetery in its many seasonal shades and moods. Often enough, there

---

[19] I only began systematic journals upon arrival in our new home, in October of 2016, and hence the story begins later in the year, in the autumn.

would be a notable found object along the path: a rosary bead, a plastic blue rose, a small cherub angel, a small Holy Mary icon. Birds, especially rooks, were constant presences, sometimes even cheekily chatting to me. A range of gravestones, from simple Roman Catholic cross motifs to Celtic Christian ornate affairs, populate the area. Some graves receive regular loving attention, whereas others are left to slowly crumble into neglectful dereliction; some have dedications "In loving memory," and an occasional one just with "In Memory."

I would sometimes wonder about my own mortality and epitaph. My instructions were to either feed me to the raptors or to ocean creatures; or, if cremation is an easy option, to disperse my ashes, perhaps into a lake or somewhere in nature, and to ponder any oracular final words.

A neglected grave stands out. Its embedded angel, of about three feet long, had fallen from the gravestone onto the ground. Some kind soul arranged it nicely, though, resting it at the grave's base. Climbing ivy — evergreen and symbolic of eternal life — tenaciously climbs its way into exquisite patterning to adorn this fallen angel.

At night-time in our new home, I would sometimes hear things from the graveyard. Were these "wailings from hell," or only the social life from large flocks of rooks? In a liminal zone of wake-sleep, I did not ponder this as a question but assumed it as some kind of otherworldly presence. I fancied it as some kind of uncanny faery song. But as time moved on, and perhaps as my rationalism on the matter firmed, this occasional soundscape receded and eventually vanished.

FISH POISONING

JOURNAL ENTRY, 2ND OF NOVEMBER 2016:

Monday evening — Halloween night. At about 11PM, I started feeling something odd whilst having a pint of Guinness with friends. Had salmon for dinner at about 7PM. Later in the night, at about 2AM, I turned and felt a spasm of sickness come over me. I got up feeling dizzy and nauseas and could hardly walk. I couldn't get out of bed the next day. Lyn had to take me to the doctor.

Apparently, salmon was most probably the culprit — my piece had gone off — gastro-entiritis! It was a New Moon in Scorpio around Halloween. It felt to me that during the night a cold wind had blown into my room from the cemetery. I felt on death's door. Scorpio is the sign of death-autumn, but is also a time of colourful, soulful leaves. This is a time when the weak, sensing they will not make it through the winter, will die off. Desires to express final life impulses — sexual urges! Moving introvertedly into oneself. I find myself invoking, once again, Asclepius/Ophiuchus, the serpent-charmer.

My nausea also reminds me of a loss of soul but also inappropriate over-indulgence. I had rich chocolate cake, pizza, mocha all in one day — ugh.

DEATH OF A FRIEND

My mother, after her divorce, was friends with an artsy Bohemian group. Two of the friends were Irish and very much looked and played the part. One of them was a bit "crazy," but full of life and spirit and very creative. For instance, he was arrested on a beach in Israel for parading naked in a public space. My mother often remarked, though, how impressed she was with him: he managed to eventually pull himself together, had a family, and the responsibility of a job, yet he also retained a vital creative spark. He was, in a strange way, a role model for my younger self.

Shortly before leaving South Africa for our new land, Ireland, I had won the only raffle in my life. The prize was a painting done by this role model friend. Simple in theme, it is of a field of yellow-gold flowers under a spacious blue sky. It exhibits an understated van Gogh luminosity. It has been part of our life throughout our years in Ireland, and it currently lives on a wall in our kitchen.

On the 18th of November, 2016, I received the news he had died from pneumonia. I had only just read the evening before that in Chinese medicine, the lungs can represent grief. This was significant, as I was suffering a lot of coughing that had begun some weeks prior to moving home. It felt like a long and lingering flu from which I didn't know if I could ever recover. I wondered if our lives were in some kind of *participation mystique*, and I thought perhaps that he might have ended up taking my place (unwittingly) with the grim reaper.

HERBIE

JOURNAL ENTRY, 28TH OF NOVEMBER 2016: (NEW MOON. MOON IN SCORPIO, SUN IN SAGITTARIUS):

Just before waking up, I dreamt of Lyn and I on the way to town (a big city like London, Dublin or Cape Town). We were planning to take public transport of some sort. There was a Saturday morning feel as we walked along. Suddenly, a car appears beside us — a kind of modern white VW beetle, with [this guy I've had a problem with] as the driver. I feel we should be enemies but Lyn is fairly friendly and talks to him. I tag along and we end up deciding to join him in the car as he needs directions to get to the city centre. I mention we hardly ever go to the city centre. Driving along the motorway, I suddenly realize the car is driving backwards. [Our driver] reckons this is normal for this car, which also has auto-pilot option. I feel a bit uncomfortable with this and so ask if he can drive the right way around, which he then does. The change is barely visible. We end up driving along together to the city centre.[20]

I have notable associations with a white VW beetle. In my twenties, my mother gave me her old white beetle as my first car. This coincided with the time of my first girlfriend. Predictably, we named the car Herbie after the lovebug film from our youth. Herbie was part of our young love lives and (according to my girlfriend's father) "miraculously" even got us across the country and back for a holiday to Cape Town. The film Herbie is relevant in that the car was rescued from a junkyard. In the film, it has red and blue stripes and a prominent number 53. Herbie has a soul and a personality and went on to achieve some remarkable feats.

Nowadays, some years on, I occasionally sight a "Herbie" VW Beetle. Whenever I do, I ponder its symbolic significance for my life context. One such notable occasion was on Friday 3rd of July, 2009, during a research trip for my PhD studies. I had been granted special permission for a Bollingen Tower visit, and also an afternoon with Jung's great grandson Andreas at the Kusnacht house to view Jung's study and peruse his alchemical books. Making sure not to be late, I arrived by train at Kusnacht station early. Over lunch near the station, I

---

[20] Of interest is that the 26th of November, 1922 was the discovery of Tutankhamen's tomb. Scarab iconography features in this major archaeological find of the 20th century. See my section on "scarabs" in chapter 2022: Judgement XX.

spotted a VW "Herbie" Beetle with stripes and the number 53 drive past. It dredged up those first girlfriend memories. Happy times, in many ways.

At this point in my PhD research, I was focusing attention on especially volume 14 of the *Collected Works*, *Mysterium Coniunctionis* ("the mysterious conjunction of opposites"). For Jung, this symbolised the culmination of an alchemical individuation process, and Jung finds correlates to notions such as the *Chymical Wedding*. Death finds archetypal amplifications as a coming-together in a wholeness. In dreams, this can be depicted as a sexual union or marriage themes. Spotting this VW "Herbie" beetle at this moment fit much of my life context at the time. Herbie, as inanimate matter animated, suggests a *coniunctio* between the organic and inorganic. Theoretically this all hints at an aspect of Jung's "mature work" around his ideas of the psychoid.

My associations to the number 53 were a bit tricky. This particular number seemed to be drawing my attention during the trip to Zurich. For instance, on the morning before taking a flight back to Dublin, on Sunday, July 5th, whilst walking along Bahnhofstrasse, I suddenly saw the number 53, and it had a snake-type sculpture next to it. Looking up, I noticed it was Mercury carved in the stone (in human form). My psyche was drawing attention to the connection between 53 and Mercury. My PhD dissertation, which I was embroiled in at the time, was titled *The Alchemical Mercurius*.

These associations are helpful in reflecting on this dream of the 28th of November, 2016, the year during which I turned 53 years of age. Perhaps there is a resonance to when Jung turned 53 years old. This was the year a remarkable synchronicity pivoted his research fully into alchemy — the aspect of his work I have always found most fascinating. Furthermore, a trip to a city in a dream can symbolise the ego-Self relationship being foregrounded and the possibility of a psychological expansion.

In terms of my partnership with Lyn, the dream symbolism could have meant being driven to a place of greater cultural relevance. The driver, materially successful, suggests it is the more sensate-driven shadow aspect of myself that is providing a dynamism to *get there*. I would later also come to appreciate the symbolism of the beetle, especially in its connotation to the scarab. In the dream, the car drives backwards, just as the scarab walks backwards when pushing a dungball — there can be more traction in this position. The scarab, amplified with Egyptian mythological references, is a quintessential symbol of rebirth and is associated especially with the heart. This Death year had strongly activated my feeling nature. The dream was also perhaps intimating that a rebirth of my life was possible and was underway, but required some navigation and integration of a more materialistic drivenness.

A BRUSH WITH DEATH

JOURNAL ENTRY, 3ʳᵈ OF JANUARY, 2017 (TUESDAY – REFLECTIONS ON THE CLOSING OF 2016):

On New Year's Eve I discovered a new path through the graveyard, the park, and to the Suir River walk. I had a lovely walk with Lyn — soulful — mid-winter — again a feeling of acceptance and a gratitude of life how it has transpired — despite the difficulties. On the way back and just after exiting the graveyard, I nearly got knocked down by a truck.

The graveyard exit is directly onto a road with a sharp, blind curb. It has taken the council a good few years to place a warning sign on the gate. I found this near-death experience disturbing and possibly a divine retribution. That New Year's Eve, I was reminiscing about my Death card year and had hubris, almost sneering at the gods that I had escaped death. The nature of this death also did not come out of the blue.

In more desperate moments of my life, I had contemplated my death in this way, by truck or by train. The immediacy appealed to me, compared to what I considered a more stretched-out saga — such as death by drowning or illness. There was some symbolism in this, the nature of death. Death by impact onto earth. For a more dreamy, intuitive nature such as mine, this could be interpreted as a wake-up call to get in touch with the grit of reality and to address the material and more sensate aspects of my life. I had waking visions of being scraped off the tarmac. In alchemical language, this would be not only a *mortificatio* but also a call toward *coagulatio*.

It was only some years later, in 2018, whilst preparing a workshop with Lyn for a Jung in Ireland event, that the value of this near-death experience became clearer. The theme for the week-long study seminar was Facing Mortality: Fear of the Unknown. As part of the preparation, we ourselves responded to the workshop brief we created, where we use words and images to depict our own experience of a near-death experience. As we've come to appreciate, based on our years of running the Jungian Psychology with Art Therapy course, such exercises can be most insightful. Jung puts it well: "Often the hands [e.g. in creating an image] will solve a mystery which the intellect has struggled with in vain."[21]

I began by using pastels and sketched out an aerial view of our home, the cemetery, the park, and the river walk. Without artistic skill or technique, a childlike playfulness took over. I found myself energised by the highly expressive imagery that began to emerge.

The image condensed a number of experiences from the many walks. Huge flocks of rooks swirled around the many gravestones; the river came alive with dangerous swirls and vortexes. At the place of the near-death experience, on the road, I drew a red splash, which evolved into a kind of five-pointed star. Our home took on an image of a dark-light with colours, as if a valuable luminosity from the depths had surfaced.

After reflecting on our experiences of the brief, we settled on the title for our workshop as Spirals of Life, Brushes with Death. The making of the image was highly satisfying (more so than my usual art-making escapades). Afterwards, reflecting on it, a key insight emerged in that the brush with death released a huge amount of life-energy that would unfold into the following years. This energy was required to help with the next leg of our alchemical opus, the pioneering of a more

---

[21] Jung, *CW* 8, par. 180.

ambitious follow-up on the Jungian Psychology with Art Therapy course. This would become the MA in Art, Psyche and the Creative Imagination programme.

2017: The High Priestess (II)

Jung in Ireland; Funerary Rite; A Piece of Coal; Black Birds;
The Good People; Petrovsky Garden; Wolf Moon

The High Priestess in the Rider-Waite Tarot deck comes after The Magician. She sits robed in light blue with a cross between her breasts, wearing a headdress as a triple Moon, with the full Moon looking like a pearl. A large yellow crescent Moon is at her left foot, and she sits at the entrance to a garden of pomegranates, with a pillar on either side of her. The pillar to her right is black with the letter B inscribed. The pillar to her left is white and has the letter J inscribed. She holds the Holy Book of the Torah, and in the Marseilles deck, the card is titled La Papesse (the Popess).

The High Priestess has been interpreted as a human embodiment of an archetypal Goddess and of women's mysteries associated with her. The Goddesses have, of course, many forms, such as Isis, Ishtar, and Astarte. A single culture would typically have many refractions of this central being — in the Western esoteric tradition, such figures would include the Virgin Mary and Sophia. The Priestess holding the Holy Book as the Torah finds parallels in paintings of Mary and the Annunciation, including the prophetic message of her as the carrier of the divine child. Psychologically, this can mean a "second birth" as a precursor to individuation.

The cross at her breast is symbolic of uniting the horizontal dimension of human everyday existence (Spirit of the Times) with the vertical spiritual and soul dimensions (Spirit of the Depths). The black and white pillars, derived from the temple of the legendary King Solomon, symbolise the refraction of consciousness into dualities (good and evil, life and death, male and female, and so on) once incarnated, compared to its more unitary nature symbolised as the original paradisal Garden.

The Lunar "Hathor" headdress depicts the Moon in waxing, full, and waning phases, which has been interpreted as three developmental phases of the feminine: girlhood, womanhood (including pregnancy and birth), and the crone or elder phase. Her connection to water is accentuated not only by the Moon, which controls the tides and some natural rhythms, but also by the watery colour and texture of her robes. In classical Jungian psychology, the High Priestess for a male can symbolise an aspect of his inner psychological feminine counterpoint, which Jung termed the *anima*. This anima figure becomes autonomously projected onto the outer world, entangling him in the destiny of his life.

JOURNAL ENTRY, 3ᴿᴰ OF JANUARY, 2017 (TUESDAY), CONTINUED:

On New Year's evening, we visited Grace Wells, with her creative and musical friends. Toward the end of the evening, I spread the Tarot deck and humorously pulled one of them out to be more prominent. No one was taking this particular card, so I decided to take it. It turned out to be The High Priestess.

The card certainly came as a relief after my Death card year.

JUNG IN IRELAND

Over the years, I had noticed a particularly enticing annual event, Jung in Ireland, run by The New York Centre for Jungian Studies. Just as I harboured a dream to one day have the resources to train as a Jungian analyst, so this also became a dream. It all looked so wonderful. However, the cost was completely out of our means, especially considering our economic implosion.

For the April 2017 event, I noticed one of our guest lecturers, Christina Mulvey, was on the faculty. I would sometimes introduce Christina to our students as the crown jewel, as one of our own course guests, as her more classical approach (having trained at the C. G. Jung Institute in Zurich) especially appealed to me. She was also highly creative in her approach, bringing in music, art, and poetry. Our chats, prior to her sessions, were always rich and soulful. On this particular occasion, though, in the lead-up to her Jung in Ireland experience, she had fallen ill. She had recommended to the New York Centre for Jungian Studies that Lyn and I be invited to fill in at short notice.

It didn't take much convincing, though we were constrained to limited participation, given that I had work commitments. The deal included a couple of nights, dinners, and breakfasts at the luxurious Connemara Coast Hotel in County Galway, as well as an invitation to attend presentations and workshops if they didn't clash with our own delivery. In exchange, we would deliver a couple of workshops.

JOURNAL ENTRY, 4TH OF APRIL, 2017 (TUESDAY):

We have just arrived back from a Jung in Ireland luxury weekend where we met writer and Jungian analyst Jean Shinoda Bolen (author of Goddesses in Everywoman*). A most wonderful octogenarian. For some reason, she activated a lot of soulful emotions in me.*

Other notable High Priestesses we had the good fortune of meeting included astrologer, writer, and Jungian analyst, Monika Wikman, as well as sacred singer, writer, and humanist priestess, Nóirín Ní Riain.

On Sunday evening (the 2nd of April), I felt touched and emotional about the whole experience.

That night, in a liminal state between wake and dream, I had a hypnagogic-like vision of being in this beautiful country house that seemed to be mine (and also my mother's) home. There was a wonderful feeling of peace, love , and acceptance. It felt like some kind of gnostic homecoming.

An earlier memory is that on our way to the weekend, on Friday morning, we noticed a rainbow in the distance ahead of us, like a gateway. Then, that afternoon as we arrived at the hotel and whilst parking the car, there was another rainbow in front of us. It was a blessed moment, and a blessed weekend.

Reflecting on my Tarot card of the year, The High Priestess, was pertinent. We had encountered at least three *women of the mysteries.* Firstly, there was Jean Shinoda Bolen. Some years back, after reading her book, *Crossing to Avalon,* I had an impression of her as a strong woman (physically, intellectually, and spiritually). It was therefore quite unusual meeting her as a little old lady in her eighties, with such a spirit that was not only serious but also girlishly mischievous. She touched my heart. She surely is a High Priestess with her sensibility of an otherworld, yet embedded in our times and speaking up about injustices in her life story of activism.

And then there was Monika Wikman, author of the book *Pregnant Darkness: Alchemy and the Rebirth of Consciousness*. Dinner with her revealed a strong kinship, an alchemist and *soror mystica* of sorts. Her presentation the following day included personal accounts of stage 4 cancer that had brought her close to death.

My third, especially notable, High Priestess of the weekend was theologian and singer-performer Nóirín Ní Riain. She introduced herself at the very beginning of the seminar in the Irish language. This touched a sensitivity for some of the American participants who became flooded with emotions.

Nóirín's presentation included autobiographical elements that were a combination of amusing and intriguing. One of her stories stood out to me. As a little girl, she would officiate a mass to her beloved soft toy animals, extending her words to the domestic and wild animals in nature.

A FUNERARY RITE

JOURNAL ENTRY, 3ᴿᴰ OF MAY, 2017 (WEDNESDAY):

On Saturday, the 29ᵗʰ of April, I had my first-ever Reiki session with a local friend who had completed our Certificate in Jungian Psychology with Art Therapy.

I was placed on a table and then various flavoured waters sprinkled on me amidst soundscapes reminiscent of sea, waves, and wind chimes. Before long, I was lulled into a deep state of relaxation. I began experiencing the visual emergence of powerful swirls of energy — as my body immersed and dissolved in a kind of liquid crystal. Occasionally, I opened my eyes — seeing this [High Priestess] weaving what seemed to be spells and incantations and movements with her hands. It reminded me of being dissolved in the tomb of the Rosarium (we had had a prior conversation about transformation from caterpillar — chrysalis — butterfly).

This all felt like some kind of Egyptian funerary rite, laid out like a corpse with all the magical carry on.

This particular image, though, resonates strongly as this month (May) my progressed Sun leaves earth sign Virgo (caterpillar phase) and finally enters air sign Libra (butterfly phase). My life had shifted firmly into the arts. This point of the progressed Sun into Libra is the autumn equinox point and so also synchronises symbolically with a tilt/swing into the underworld of the Am Duat of ancient Egyptian mythology.

Progressed Sun moving into Libra, the scales, had an Egyptian mythological reference as being "weighed in the scales of Ma'at" at the threshold of the afterlife. I was being inducted into a new phase of my life, having died to my previous self. This Reiki ritual brought the symbolism home in an embodied way, and so it had a synchronistic resonance.

The image of the *Amduat*, passage through the Egyptian underworld, had made an impression on me ever since meeting Jungian analyst and author Andreas Schweizer. Some years back, during my trip to Zurich with the purpose of visiting Jung's Bollingen Tower and his library (of alchemical texts) at his home at Kusnacht, Andreas suggested we meet at the Psychological Club, and then have a coffee at a nearby café.

I am usually very punctual. On this occasion, though, I found myself getting lost in the many streets, trying to find the Psychological Club. Being hot, sweaty, and tired, with the angst of being late, was beginning to weigh me down. Street names such as Neptunestrasse, Merkurstrasse, and Minervastrasse added to what was becoming a delirium in a kind of mythical maze. Eventually, perhaps fifteen minutes late, I finally arrived at the Psychological Club.

Below ground level, down a staircase, I saw what must have been the caretaker locking up. After exchanging a few words, this turned out to be Andreas Schweizer. I found this initial meeting symbolically noteworthy: Andreas as a gatekeeper of an "underworld." Upon meeting, he functioned as a psychopomp and kindly showed me around the Psychological Club, elaborating a few quaint anecdotes, such as the three thrones at the front of the hall. Apparently, these were for Jung, Emma, and Toni Wolff during lectures and events at the club. Later, over a coffee, Andreas mentioned his upcoming book publication, *The Sun God's Journey through the Netherworld: Reading the Ancient Egyptian Amduat*. The symbolism of this title in relation to our first meeting felt synchronistic. The cover of this book features an embalmed figure on a table with its bird-like *ba*-soul hovering above. It depicts a transformation mystery, from sarcophagus/chrysalis to winged being. This image appeared to me during my Reiki session just mentioned, reinforcing the symbolism of my life moving from the death of a previous identity and toward a new life, with the High Priestess as psychopomp.

It also brought to mind a piece relating to Jung's death, which I had developed as part of my PhD and subsequent book publication on the *Alchemical Mercurius*. To quote, including excerpts from Bair's biography, from the concluding part of my chapter on Hermeticism:

> The story, to be found in Bair's recent biography relates that shortly after Jung's death his daughter Marianne organised the making of a death mask for the purpose of a bust. Stoiber, the local specialist commissioned for the task, remarked that Jung's corpse was 'so impressive' and that on his forehead were three lines, 'like a triton,' a pattern similar to some she had seen in India on the faces of Ra, the Sun god.' Stoiber's unique ritualistic method, after taking a plaster cast, was to then infuse it with a combination of beeswax, resins and incense 'for symbolic reasons.' She chose beeswax because of its 'certain meaning, immortality for example' and the bee as 'a symbol of the pharaoh'. For the cast, although not knowing much about Jung, she selected 'brown with lots of red', sensing that 'he was a very earthy man besides his spirituality and he had a good relationship to stone.'
>
> The description is evocative of an ancient Egyptian funerary rite. In particular, the triton on Jung's forehead might be interpreted as his being touched by the three-pronged golden wand of the thrice-great Egyptian Hermes, as the "lord of the night" and "sender of oracles" whose wand can bestow both life and death.[22]

A PIECE OF COAL

This transformation, from Virgo-Earth to Libra-Air, correlates to the Equinox axes of the yearly round. Like Yang beginning to change to Yin, the scales begin to tip. Daylight begins to slowly decrease, with every new day up to the winter solstice, when the darkness gradually increases.

---

[22] Mathew Mather, *The Alchemical Mercurius: Esoteric Symbol of Jung's Life and Works* (London: Routledge, 2014), 25.

Our second annual Art and Psyche Symposium was titled 'Creative Imagination and the Symbolic Life'. Julie Aldridge gave an inspiring talk on Art and Alchemy, followed by mine on Jung's Red Book. Our third speaker of the day was Lucy Dolan on 'Light and Dark' as a numinous story of her clay coniunctio sculpture in St Brigid's garden in Galway. After lunch, Lucy and I co-facilitated an 'Art, synchronicity and myth-making' workshop.

The workshop required participants to pick a random natural object hidden in packets (Lucy had sourced some of these from her locale in Ventry). On impulse, I decided to also draw a 'random' object from Lucy's packets. It was a piece of coal that had been smoothed by the sea.

My first reaction was one of controlled shock. The immediate association was that Santa had brought me a piece of coal for being a bold boy. A piece of hell coal during the first day of my Nekyia. My associations revolved around an expectation that I should have been included in my father's will, and that I was now being punished (or were) by the ancestral realm of the fathers.

An optimistic association, though, is that of a substance that can evolve into a diamond over aeons of time. Coal as a nigredo *state and also a* prima materia *(of sorts) with the possibility of transmutation.*

Lucy had found this piece of coal on Ventry beach, near Dingle, on the westernmost part of Ireland. Over the years, we had many a family summer holiday on this beach, in a caravan with no electricity. On one of these holidays, I read a local book titled *The Dingle Diamond,* which colourfully elaborated a local mystique of this area steeped in myth, religion, spirituality, and pilgrimage. Enchanted by this spectacularly beautiful landscape, I often refer to it as my spiritual home.

Receiving a piece of coal as a "gift of the fathers" in this uncanny way, considering the workshop title, took on the charge of a symbol. Negatively, it reflected being punished by fathers. Positively, it hinted at a concentrated energy that could allow for an alchemical transformation: the energy retrieved from a deeper strata of psyche that could fuel a creative ambition. As they say, necessity is the mother of invention. In the midst of our financial fallout, this was a most helpful symbol. It allowed an intensity and passion to be proactive about navigating a career toward a deeper engagement with creativity and psyche. It also gave further impetus to progressing the notion of a Master's degree in Art, Psyche and the Creative Imagination.

BLACK BIRDS

On Wednesday, the 19th of July, 2017, I got an email notification from our librarian of the arrival of a book I had ordered, some weeks prior, titled *Songlines of the Soul: Pathways to a New Vision for a New Century,* by Veronica Goodchild. An image of a crop circle mandala with the motif of a hummingbird appears on the front cover.

That same evening, we had our friend Grace Wells over for dinner to discuss the prospect of a significant venture inspired, in part, by our experiences in Galway. An excerpt from some of the notes I had compiled in preparation for the meeting read as follows:

> "Its vision is to host experiential study seminars in spectacular environments, steeped in historical and mythopoeic significance. A celebration of life, it combines spirit of place, luxury accommodation, gourmet food and an inner-outer exploration of myth, art and psyche. Led by leading cultural creatives, it aims to bring a diversity of individuals together in rare opportunities of sharing. We engage in questions that matter — of both personal and cultural significance. We breathe life into learning, and dare to envision a new dreaming."

That night, after a lovely evening of sharing and conversation, I had a particularly moving dream. One of those rare spiritual dreams: Lyn and I were part of this experiment that involved the possibility of hatching birds. It turned out the experiment was doing unexpectedly well. Someone told us to go and check as our birds were now hatching. It was twilight (early morning or evening) and we had to go outside and up a bit to a kind of chimney. Putting our hands into the chimney, there was this exquisite sensation of all these beautiful, soft baby birds — a very spiritual feeling, really lovely. They might have been Starlings? Or Blackbirds? We helped them to fly free into the sky — a cute and loving feeling. They had miraculously grown from newly hatched to fairly confident flyers within a few moments.

The following evening, on the 20th of July, I phoned a friend in London who shared my Jungian interests. In discussing the dream, he amplified it by mentioning the medieval *Mutus Liber* image of alchemist and *soror mystica* in front of the alchemical oven in prayerful dedication to their opus. This was useful in that it felt as though my piece of coal (a symbol that had developed significant importance from previous dreams and synchronicities) had been worked upon and sublimated from its dark (*nigredo*) state to a multiplication (*multiplicatio*) into many birds. My friend also mentioned the chimney in terms of an archetypal cosmic umbilical chord, a connection between our earthly world and a transcendent realm above.

In further exploring the dream, I recalled a number of memories. A notable one is that every spring, when we lived in the Nire Valley, and for a number of years, we'd hear scuffles of jackdaws who had stubbornly nested in the chimney. Efforts to pull all their twigs, sheep's wool, and once an egg out of the chimney in hopes of encouraging them to move along were in vain. Some years, we just gave up and allowed them to settle in for the summer. They let out sporadic chirpings that at times escalated into raucous family squabbling, and I would joke about listening to them as my advisors whilst working in our kitchen on my PhD thesis.

The notion of an alchemist's oven also has strong personal associations. In our stone cottage in the valley, Lyn and I would sometimes sit during cold and wintry evenings by the open fire of our kitchen wood stove, sharing dreams, images, memories and ideas whilst enjoying dinner and sipping on wine, port, or a whisky. We also had the rich material of our students' soul-work to dwell upon and discuss.

One such evening in autumn, perhaps due to too much detritus left behind from our bird family, the fire started becoming rather lively. Within minutes, it was clear the chimney had caught fire. Fortunately, though, we got the situation under control without too much drama, thanks also to the kind hospitality of our neighbours.

It was thus with a rich personal symbolic context that this bird dream could be appreciated. Much of the dream made sense retrospectively, in light of Lyn and me and our soul-project, the Jungian Psychology with Art Therapy course. We had helped to nurture and hatch "soul eggs" — helping others to awaken a wisdom of the heart (*cardiognosis*). Our hermetic birds were hatching. And now, with the new project on the horizon, the possibility of developing an MA degree, it was perhaps also prospective of further endeavours.

Two days on, on Saturday the 20th of July, I continued reading *Songlines of the Soul*. In the first chapter, I read of a dream the author had of a holy man she identified as a Tibetan monk who, just before dying, expressed happiness that he had managed to save and liberate his son, whom he gave to the dreamer to take care of.

After the dream, Veronica (the author) decided to engage in an active imagination to find out more about this holy man. In a quiet meditative state, she began. Suddenly, a bird started singing an otherworldly song. After a while, the holy man and the bird merged and became one. When Veronica then asked the bird who he was, it answered that it was Suhrawardi — the name of a twelfth-century Sufi mystic. After the active imagination, she managed to locate the mystic in one of her books. It turned out that one of Suhrawardi's projects included a short book, *The Treatise of the Birds*. It is the story of a journey of the soul into the visionary landscape of the *mundus imaginalis* — a beautiful imaginal city atop a mountain. She further noted that Suhrawardi had insisted on the *really real* (ontologically valid) nature of such otherworldly places. Followers of his mystery school identified themselves as "the people of love."

I found this excerpt striking, as it added another dimension to my bird dream. It felt like an invitation to a new frontier. The black birds in my dream, with their fluttering, were akin to love sensations toward a greater awakening of the heart.

A couple of days later, Monday, the 22nd of July, occurred more experiences that reaffirmed such a reading of the situation. A friend of mine invited me to meet at a local café around lunchtime. About halfway on my walk down to town, I stumbled upon part of a hatched bird's egg along my path, and so picked it up.

Over lunch, we talked about Tibetan Buddhism. He related that he ended up settling with the Shambhala school. I also mentioned my bird dream and the eggshell. He then told me of a friend of his who, a fair while back, had given him this whole box of different wild birds' eggs that were lying around for ages, getting all muddled up and broken. It got me thinking of my birds hatching from my dream, and so wondered about persuading him to gift me his birds' eggs collection. They could come in handy for one of our workshops on synchronicity. After our lunch, I returned home and continued reading *Songlines of the Soul,* having progressed now to part IV of the book, on "Mystical Cities." Here I read a whole section on Shambhala. Rather curious, I thought, in light of having just had a discussion with my friend on Shambhala and Tibetan Buddhism.

Overall, the arrival of this fresh perspective, a few days after my bird dream, thus constituted a synchronicity. It appeared to function as an invitation to expand my own worldview, to venture forth into an exploration of the *mundus imaginalis.*

THE GOOD PEOPLE

At a local event hosted at an old-world guesthouse, Lyn and I attended an evening with the great Irish *Senachai* (storyteller) Eddie Lenihan. Some years back, Eddie was embroiled in an issue that erupted into world news. It was about a Hawthorn bush in the middle of a planned highway. Both Hawthorn and Blackthorn, as sister trees, are revered trees of Ireland, renowned for their connection to "The Other Crowd," more commonly known as the faeries. Another name Eddie mentions, based on his gathering of local folklore, is "The Good People." On this occasion of storytelling, towards the beginning of the evening, the chandelier lights in the room began to flicker, unexpectedly, with no conjuring trick suspected. Even Eddie was speechless, his gift of the gab failing to come up with a humorous or enchanting quip. It appeared to me the rationalist worldview had won the moment, with the audience and Eddie seemingly passing the transient event off as nonsense, a superstition, and faulty electrics.

Having lived in an old stone cottage in the heart of the beautiful Nire valley in Ireland for some years made me less suspicious. I had a collection of anomalous experiences that would suggest Other presences. For instance, the land we lived on was in the path of a nearby boreen (old rural pathway) just above. It aligns with the outhouses, as we came to realise in times of floods when water flowed down this path. My experiences included unusual dreams, as well as hearing joyful children's voices, laughing, and wild parties at certain times and places. There were also more unsettling experiences that contributed to the decision to move to town.[23]

I had often pondered all of this and tended to oscillate between psychological interpretations and the notion of an ontically real parallel realm that had (meaningful) touch points with our world. In the latter view, it seems that this Other realm has affinities with a very different notion from the positivist scientific Western worldview.

Perhaps some of the older (folkloric) ways had learnt to work with this uncanny realm, to induce phenomena such as miracle healing and also a form of magic to effect justice beyond the institutional strictures of a hierarchical society. These also included visits to the local Cailleach, the village representative of the divine hag, as officiator of such feats, and mediator of the ancestral.

JOURNAL ENTRY, 14TH OF JULY, 2017 (FRIDAY):

A couple of days ago, on the 12th of May, Lyn and I decided to fetch water from a lesser-known holy spring on mountain road. An inconvenient spot, tricky for parking our car due to a steep incline as well as a sharp blind corner. After encountering quite a few stony steps into the forest, we reached the spring, surrounded by a craggy, hand-made stone wall. There was a

---

[23] Stories for another time and place.

Hawthorn tree next to it, decorated with wishing rags. Lyn took golden (or silver!) threads from her scarf, which we tied into the tree. We made our wishes, as is the custom. She reminded me that she also did this at our Nire valley home, of tying rags onto our hawthorn tree next to our house (this was the month my father was dying, back in 2013). During this excursion I started getting revelations about the nature of 'The Other Crowd' and our relationship to them.

I pondered that perhaps the multiverse theory, at least in part, was right. An overarching, meaningful interpenetration of worlds. This notion would require an extension of the Jungian archetypal perspective and of our understanding of a transpersonal unconscious.

I realised one can invoke this world in times of stress to redress a karmic imbalance when human institutional structures have failed. This can give a more positive valence as to our dealings and understandings of this Otherworld in relation to ours.

I noticed in my dream life the rare occasion of the erotic. These included an unknown, enigmatic faery woman who seemed to coincide with my creative life — being true to a calling, without the usual necessary compromises derived from super-ego type fears, such as "what would the academy think about this?" Being true to the perspective I had developed in my PhD and subsequent book on Mercurius meant adhering to the question of *Liber Novus* as a new book for our times? I hold the notion that the erotic faery woman is a particular personification of the *Anima Mundi* (Soul of the World) in a unique relation to my life. A being "more real than real," another aspect of the Cailleach, a High Priestess of sorts.

JOURNAL ENTRY, 16TH OF JULY 2017 (SUNDAY):

Dreamt of being by the sea, swimming in lovely warmish green-turquoise waves with a couple of others. A sense of a childhood holiday by a seaside village. Suddenly, out of the sea, this very large train emerged. Two carriages with a height of perhaps a three-storey house (though no sense of it having levels). Old-fashioned in style but not spewing out smoke. It was a beautiful turquoise and lilac colour.

Quite a spectacle — numinous! It emerged from the sea on our left and then came around on the track to stop at the station. None of this, for some reason, seemed out of the ordinary. We were to catch this train. A lovely feeling.

In my journal, I noted two associations. The first was of an old man storyteller living in a Gypsy caravan from the film

Into the West. Toward the end of the film, the young boys on their stolen horse eventually arrive on the west coast of Ireland. The horse goes rogue and enters the waves of the sea, plunging the boys into a dangerous encounter. The old man, agonised by the effect of his stories on the young lads, reflects on the wild waves of the sea being kin to the horses of the sea god Manannán mac Lir (King of the Otherworld, and one of the magical peoples of Irish myth, the Tuatha Dé Danann), arriving to take them into his oceanic underworld.

My second association was of an account from a book I had been reading, Eddie Lenihan's *Meeting The Other Crowd*, about a faery funeral and the death carriage being of an inordinate size — about the size of the train in my dream.

A further excerpt from my journal:

> *I wonder if this dream might have something to do with our work toward developing the MA in Art, Psyche and the Creative Imagination? Inside the train carriage, there was a sense of a faery banquet. The train could hook up further carriages, as if there could be a rich haul. There was a sense of immense energy, and perhaps good fortune coming our way. Time to take the Kairos moment.*

The dream reflected a rupture of ordinary life and the appearance of an Otherworldly phenomenon emerging from the sea. The feeling was that there was no time to lose. We should *catch the train* before it leaves the station. It gave an affirmation for the big thing going on in our lives at the time; to respond to the unique opportunity of the moment, to further the MA aspiration.[24] This venture aligned with the ethos and values of a new and hopeful era. A small yet valuable contribution within a grand unfolding dynamic. Instead of a funeral or death, it had the feeling of an archetypal new beginning. In terms of the Aquarian Age, linked to innovation and humanitarian values, it was a symbol of inevitable momentum toward a new era.

---

[24] Some years later, in 2023, my PhD student Lisa Hester, working on Re-envisioning Visionary Art, introduced me to the work of visionary artist Amanda Sage. Her work *Great Wave of Trainsformation*, made in 2020-21, has similarities to my dream.

Petrovsky Garden

Journal entry, 24ᵗʰ of July, 2017 (Monday):

Back home, I continue reading Songlines of the Soul *about celestial cities, including the Tibetan Shambhala! In one passage, we read of a description of a 'perfected world where everything — lotus, dragonfly, waters — is itself a teaching of liberation, freedom, and enlightenment. But one of the main keys to attainment of this state is mastery of the subtle body.'[25]*

Yesterday, at the garden (Petrovsky garden), we watched two dragonflies (and bees) in a pond with Lotus flowers.

In this enchanted garden, my friend, a practitioner of Vajrayana Buddhism, mentioned to me about the heart of the earth itself being a meditating Buddha.

Quoting the book I was reading: 'In "The Emerald Tablet of Thoth" ... an inscription beautifully reads: "deep in the Earth's heart lies the flower, the source of the Spirit that binds all in its form. For know ye that the Earth is living in body as though art alive in thine own form The Flower of Life is as thine own place of Spirit, and streams forth through the Earth as thine flows through thy form."'

This journal entry touches on sacred spaces: one as a mythical, celestial city of Shambhala (an above), and the other being in the heart of the earth (a below). These motifs constellated in a synchronistic way around the time of — and during — this Sunday visit to Petrovsky garden near our hometown of Clonmel. In the Rider-Waite Tarot deck, the High Priestess is at the entrance of a secret garden. A spirit of place, and associated knowledge, allowed for a mystical experience and pointed toward a wisdom tradition that would have charted such a territory more substantially. The book *Songlines of the Soul* was a key to its revealing.

Wolf Moon

Journal entry, 31ˢᵀ of December, 2017 (Sunday):

Been so busy ... finally a chance to catch up a bit on journal. My favourite weather of mist and rain, sitting next to the sliding door in Lyn's art room and enjoying the rainy day mood and good feeling having finished an unex-

---

[25] Veronica Goodchild, *Songlines of the Soul: Pathways to a New Vision for a New Century* (Boston: Nicolas-Hays Inc, 2012), 236.

pected project in time for the New Year 2018 and the Supermoon Full Moon, as the Wolf Moon, 1st of January 2018.

The unexpected project arose from a meeting of my postgraduate research student (looking at animation director Tomm Moore's films Secret of Kells (2009), Song of the Sea (2014) and his upcoming, Wolfwalkers), with Tomm Moore and myself.[26] Tomm requested to see us on the 19th of December at his studio in Kilkenny.

During our chat he brought up the topic of their current film Wolfwalkers, which would be the third in his triptych, and asked if I could take a look at the completed animatic with a view to devising Jungian and mythological commentary.

I ended up immersing myself in this project, even some time on Xmas day, and eventually finished a 5500 word Jungian commentary — ready to email off on the New Year, which coincided with a Wolf Moon!

The Wolf Moon is one of a Triptych of Super Moons (3rd of December 2017, 1st of January 2018, and the 31st of January 2018) in which the 3rd is a Blue Moon as well as a Lunar eclipse.. A 'Blue Blood' Moon.

I include an excerpt from my commentary below. The Lunar emphasis fits the symbolism in the Rider-Waite Tarot of the High Priestess, wearing a headdress depicting the three phases of the Moon.

WOLF LAIR (OPENING IMAGE)

The opening image can be considered a seed-symbol that captures much of the essence of the story. Here we see a 'Madonna and child' enshrined within a wolf's lair. More broadly, it is comprised of a Trinitarian feminine — daughter, mother, grandmother, where grandmother is the archetypal Great Mother (Mother Nature). Like a Russian doll, they are enclosed successively within each other and cradled in the womb of nature. Their expressions are enigmatic and reminiscent of a bodhisattva-like deep meditation. The golden torc-like earrings, wheel badge, spiral and circular motifs suggest a Celtic royal lineage. The soft, luxurious and floral lair conveys a holiness — once the birthplace of the wolf-child, protected by an outer ring of fearsome wolves. Her hair is like a halo. A larger perspective of the scene reveals a waterfall, small lake, and river. It is a cornucopia of invigorating life-energy: pouring endlessly from the Celtic otherworld. The aesthetic of a soft exquisite watercolour style, with the nuance and subtlety of hand-drawn, reveals a soul-like quality of nature suffused by the

---

[26] All three films won numerous awards as well as Oscar nominations. Wolfwalkers came out in November 2020.

sacred. It resonates with a deeper mythopoeic layer, a nostalgic sweet spot, of a Celtic spirituality.

This holy lair is in a forest in Ireland, land of the Goddess. Here we are introduced to one of the main protagonists of the story — a green-eyed, red-haired, feral, and spirited little girl named Mebh, who embodies much of the soul of Ireland. Her life and forest community are under radical threat. Historically, it is a time when Cromwell and his army are conquering Ireland, killing and enslaving its people, destroying its forests, and exterminating wolf populations.

In hindsight, we can see how some of the year, punctuated by synchronistic phenomena, played out around the theme of the High Priestess. All of this helped to reorient my values and worldview more fully into one that is soulful, fluid, and changeable. The High Priestess, as an expression of the *Anima Mundi*, was refracted into a number of especially female influences in my life.

2018: THE FOOL (O)

Joker card; The Fool's Bag; Caduceus; Pilgrim Dream; Ishtar and Ophiuchus; Sheela-na-gig; The Cathedral and the Fool; Blue Butterfly

The Fool in the Tarot is card o, the "joker in the pack." The Rider-Waite deck depicts him as a carefree soul wandering on a mountaintop with his head in the sky and the Sun brightly at the top right. In the distance, we see snow-capped mountains. He is at a cliff-edge and seemingly about to fall to his peril. His small white dog tries to draw his attention to the impending danger. In his right hand, he carries a staff at the end of which is a bag. Presumably, these are his worldly possessions, or perhaps tools to help his survival. In his left hand, he carries a white rose. On his green floral tunic are a number of eight-pointed red stars (or spokes or flowers) in yellow or golden-filled circles. In the Marseille deck, the Fool is on level ground with staff and bag, and a walking stick in his right hand. His small dog is biting his right buttock, with pants torn. A variation on this card has the Fool following a butterfly.[27] He tends to fall down the occasional (alchemical) rabbit hole.

The Fool, as a shapeshifter, can take on any value in the Major Arcana, with the capacity of breaking the rules of our taken-for-granted reality. He finds expression through anomalous phenomena such as synchronicities. Sallie Nichols provides a rather colourful description:

> His energy is unconscious and undirected, yet it seems to have a purpose of its own. He moves outside space and time. The winds of prophecy and poesy inhabit his spirit. Although he wanders with no fixed abode, he endures intact throughout the ages. His multicoloured costume spins a rainbow wheel, offering us glimpses into eternity. As patterns in a kaleidoscope appear and disappear, so the Fool pops in and out of our world."[28]

---

[27] Specifically, see Il Matto (The Fool) in the 19th century Vergnano Tarot. , from the Piemontese tradition. Lothar Teikemeier, "Tarot Wheel," accessed October 2, 2025, www.tarotwheel.net

[28] Nichols, *Jung and Tarot: An Archetypal Journey*, 26.

In the medieval royal court, the Fool naively seems to have access to truths beyond the ken of the court. In a related vein, Marie-Louise von Franz writes:

> A medium is a person who has a closer relationship, one might say a gift, by which to relate to the absolute knowledge of the unconscious, generally by having a relatively low level of consciousness. This explains why mediums are often very queer and often morally odd people — not always, but often — or they are slightly criminal, or take to drink, and so on. They are generally very endangered personalities because they have that low threshold and are so near to the absolute knowledge of the unconscious.[29]

In Jungian psychology, the Fool finds expression in the figure of the alchemical Mercurius. Jung has described Mercurius in multifarious ways throughout his corpus. As a "paradox par excellence," he/she combines all conceivable opposites into his/her being. As "spirit of the unconscious" he/she is the dynamism behind the process of individuation, a journey toward becoming more whole and more conscious. In *The Spirit Mercurius*, Jung describes this figure as "the very qualities we so urgently need to heal the split in ourselves."[30]

The Fool has a kinship with the *Puer* figure of the young Greek Hermes — young, irresponsible, and flighty but filled with creative potential and spirit. In contrast, the Magician card would have stronger affinities to the matured ancient/*senex*, as the mythical Egyptian Hermes Trismegistus. In the grail legend, the Fool is the naïve Parzival, destined to play a pivotal role in restoring the wasteland of the ailing grail King to fertility and abundance.

Such depictions are quite different from portrayals in popular culture of the sad and tragic figure of The Joker from Batman and various horror-tricksters, whose idiosyncratic origins and character tend to be more rooted in psychopathology than in the archetypal figure of the divine jester.

---

[29] Marie-Louise von Franz, *On Divination and Synchronicity: The Psychology of Meaningful Chance* (Toronto: Inner City Books, 1980), 39.

[30] Jung, *Alchemical Studies*, CW 13, par. 295.

New Year's Eve leading up to 2018 was just a small gathering of five of us. I had brought the Tarot cards, though I began having second thoughts about this party trick ritual — at least the way I was doing it. The prospect of a single card as the year's theme was not necessarily so heartening if this card turned out to be The Devil, or Death, as I had come to realise. Nevertheless, it was too late to backtrack, and so I gave some cautionary preamble.

After separating out the Major Arcana, shuffling, and then laying out the cards, I invited our friends to pick a card. The Hierophant; The Empress; Judgement. Lyn picked Death. I picked The High Priestess (again) — she had not finished having her way with me! Upon some reflection, in light of a decision to perform a 22-year engagement with the Major Arcana, I decided to draw a second card: The Fool.

This New Year's Day coincided with a super Wolf Full Moon. The Lunar, divine feminine (High Priestess) was in prominence.[31] In my case, this was coupled with The Fool. This couple-ship had an echo to that first romantic past, of falling in love with an older woman as an awkward teenager. An astrological prediction had foretold it. Unusual dreams had ignited me to follow the tracks down the rabbit hole of a mysterious alchemical adventure.

JOURNAL ENTRY, 2ND OF JANUARY, 2018 (TUESDAY):

This evening, after reading The Quantum Astrologer's Handbook *by Michael Brooks (about a 17th-century gambler and mathematician Jerome Cardano), I resumed reading* The Hero's Journey *by Joseph Campbell, to recap on Parzival as the Fool.*

On New Year's day, I had decided (how could I not!) to email my Jungian commentary on Wolfwalkers to director Tomm Moore. I realized it was 10:36 AM, and so waited a few seconds to email it off for 10:37 (137 ... plus a 0 – the Fool).[32] By 11:08AM Tomm Moore already replied, very appreciative.

I find it soothing to read about Jerome Cardano's colourful 17th-century life, mostly in Milan, Italy. Talking to a guardian angel spirit in his prison (the

---

[31] Consider the variations, as The Hierophant, and The Empress tarot cards.

[32] For the significance of the number 137 for especially quantum physics see the book *137: Jung, Pauli and the Pursuit of a Scientific Obsession* (2010) by Arthur I. Miller.

author claims to be this spirit!). He advises Jerome Cardano about his life
(and happens to have some foreknowledge, living in the 21st century).33

> *This got me wondering about a guardian angel and perhaps, apart from*
> *one's Self in a Jungian sense, about ancestral spirits. helping to "look out for*
> *one." Perhaps this is the inner voice I should be learning to trust!*

Reflecting on my life, I had thought my apprenticeship to The Fool was past tense, considering six years of intense PhD research on the alchemical Mercurius, that divine jester. Its presence, though, was still alive and well. I had identified with a Holy Fool of sorts, especially considering the precarious journey our lives had become. Our situation, having economically imploded, had catapulted us into a state of grace. The currents of life, though, were kind and seemed to invisibly guide and orient us in a direction that mattered. Our Jung with Art Therapy course was thriving (we would run two cohorts in the coming academic year). The MA aspiration was also beginning to have traction. My lecturer job as side-kick, being co-programme chair in the college's Bachelor of Science (Honours) degree in Digital Animation Production, would begin to give way to full-time immersion into all things Art and Psyche; the intensification of an alchemical opus.

JOKER CARD

Having picked The Fool got me reminiscing about an earlier watershed moment from some years prior, in 2005. Around this time, at the age of 42, I was suffering the proverbial mid-life crisis, and the urge to change or reinvent my career was becoming ever stronger. Fortuitously, I had discovered there was a place in England that offered post-graduate studies on Jung. The possibility of studying in an area of my greatest interest was most alluring. During the summer of 2005, whilst at work, I decided I might as well coincide an email query with Jung's birthday (the 26th of July), and so sent

---

33 The author, Michael Brooks, is a quantum physicist. In part, his book elucidates the origins of Quantum Theory by considering the dubious life of gambler Jerome Cardano. He credits Cardano as the originator of statistics and, by extension, also quantum theory.

an email to Roderick Main, a lecturer at the centre, expressing an interest in pursuing a PhD thesis on the figure of the alchemical Mercurius.

After sending the email, I phoned Lyn and suggested we meet for lunch at Angela's, our favourite local café. After parking the car and joining her, we walked along toward the café. On the way, we stumbled across some playing cards splayed randomly on the ground outside the Friary of St Francis of Assisi. The one I picked up, which was face down, turned out to be the Joker. Uncannily the various events of the day — the email query, Jung's birthday, the Joker card, the Friary of St Francis, and the name Angela — all constellated around themes associated with the alchemical Mercurius, a divine jester precluded from the House of God. I understood this synchronicity as an affirmation that I was on the right path. In difficult moments along this challenging journey, over the course of a few years, I would contemplate this encouraging moment.

In the scraps of time I could find over the following year, I energetically worked on a PhD proposal on the alchemical Mercurius. After a number of revisions, Roderick finally suggested we meet in person at the university. It so happened that the timing, once again, constellated around Jung's birthday. However, to be precise, our in-person meeting occurred the day before, on the 25th of July, 2006.

That afternoon, in Roderick's office, we discussed the possibility of PhD research. About an hour or so into the discussion, the phone rang. Whilst Roderick chatted, I perused my notebook in an attempt to clarify and refresh some thoughts. After putting the phone down, he asked if I had heard of Robert Aziz, author of *Jung on Religion and Synchronicity,* as he was the one on the phone.

I replied that I had just that very moment read a quote in Roderick's book where he had summarised some of Robert Aziz's insights on synchronicity, which I had transcribed by hand into my notebook. In fact, my finger was still on the quote.

The synchronistic event refers to the synchronicity as experienced by ego consciousness in space and time. Here what is a unitary event in the unconscious has been refracted into multiple contexts in consciousness, so that the components of the synchronicity are experienced as separated in time and space as well as differentiated into psychic and physical events.[34]

I passed my notebook to Roderick, who, after a few ponderous moments, replied that he considered this to be a synchronicity. As a specialist on the subject of synchronicity himself, this certainly boded well for my project. On this hopeful note, I returned to Ireland to make a few final adjustments to the proposal.

Destiny had played me a card, a Joker card. I followed through by developing a proposal and by organising the time and energy, amidst a family and professional job, to embark on a life-changing journey of following the tracks of a divine jester as the alchemical Mercurius. It would be a challenging time of being "immersed in the Mercury" (of the wise) as "the highest mystery." Its playful and sometimes pernicious wiles would lead me into an adventure of psyche, revealing depths of mystery, intrigue, and sometimes threatening madness. My being and worldview would be subverted, challenged and ultimately transformed.

And then, some years later, on New Year's Day of 2018, I picked The Fool. The journey would continue.

The Fool's Bag

I first met Richard Berengarten at a Holistic Conference hosted at the University of Essex over September the 8th, 9th, and 10th, in 2017. He was the keynote speaker that first evening on the topic of his poetic engagement with the Chinese oracular book of changes, the *I Ching*. Having just registered for the conference, I ambled about, looking for old friends and also a place to sit. It turned out the only chair available happened to be at Richard's table, so I ended up sit-

---

34 Roderick Main, *The Rupture of Time: Synchronicity and Jung's Critique of Modern Western Culture* (New York: Routledge, 2004), 53.

ting next to him. I recognised him, as I had just been looking at his various poetry books on the sales table (one of them had a photograph of him on the cover). Thanks to our shared interest in synchronicity, it didn't take long to spark up a lively discussion. And so began a "strange attractor" for the duration of the conference: unplanned meetings over drinks and bumping into each other spontaneously. At some point, I mentioned that we occasionally hosted events back in Ireland and asked if he'd be interested in being a speaker at one of these. Richard responded enthusiastically.

Back in Ireland, we followed up on this idea. The event was finalised as A Divinatory Sensibility — Consulting the Oracle, to be held at the Absolute Hotel in Limerick, on Sunday, the 14th of January, 2018. Being mid-winter, and given the treacherous weather and frequent storms of the season, the time often made us question the viability of the event. Thanks to Richard's encouragement, though, we decided to proceed. The day would fall within the auspicious first New Moon (a conjunction of Sun and Moon in Capricorn) of the New Year. This is the Lunar crone phase, often associated with divination and augury, and so it seemed an appropriate time. It was also close to the New Year.

Our worries were unfounded. The day, with about thirty-five people present, went very well and consisted of Richard's talk, lunch, a presentation on Augurs, Omens, and Oracles by our local Irish poet Grace Wells, followed by a Consulting the Oracle workshop facilitated by Lyn and me.[35] During the afternoon workshop, we each selected a random natural object hidden in a small box. The objects' occultation was intended as a means of bracketing off any rational or causal influences. The choice to use objects from nature allowed for a meditative reconnection to the natural world, but also to a more esoteric sensibility as an engagement with the *anima mundi*. This gesture toward a divinatory "throwing of the bones" all seemed so outré in contrast to the plush, executive-like, clean, and

---

[35] This workshop was a variation on the one already mentioned in the previous chapter on The High Priestess, when I ended up with a piece of coal.

efficient (phallogocentric) four-star hotel environment. The objects also recall the Fool's bag, especially if we amplify this notion to include such ideas as medicine bags, crane bags, and so forth.

Many an otherworldly and potentially life-changing experience was spawned on that day. These, in part, could be considered refractions from Richard's impressive blue butterfly synchronicity story, which he recounted at our Limerick event. Following the blue butterfly as muse led him into the heart of darkness of Nazi atrocities in Yugoslavia. This was intriguing for me as in the Vergnano Tarot the Fool is enchanted by a butterfly. Prompted by Richard, I too got enchanted, and wrote an essay of his experiences. It plunged me into the horrific dimensions of humanity.

CADUCEUS

On the Super Blue Full Moon eclipse of 31st of January, I got a request from my Jungian friend Steve Myers to review his upcoming book. The front cover of this draft copy sported a *caduceus* — two serpents entwined along a central rod. His book title is *Myer's-Briggs Typology versus Jungian Individuation: Overcoming One-sidedness in Self and Society*.

The two serpents are sometimes depicted as Solar and Lunar, implying a contrariness yet also a complementarity. A reference here is the *caduceus* (herald's wand) of Hermes/Mercury. In one story, the wand was used to disentangle two snakes in combat, adding to its symbolism of bringing peace between enemies. The Fool's staff might be amplified by this reference, as well as Moses's magical staff (bringing water in the desert, parting the Red Sea), and also the healing and raising of the dead by means of the rod of Asclepius.[36]

A friend of ours, a day or two after this, posted an image from National Geographic of two entwined snakes. A cobra

---

[36] A notable childhood memory is of a wilderness holiday at the Golden Gate National Park where our guide used a staff" for catching snakes under rocks. On the occasion he took our group out he foolishly got bitten by a semi-poisonous snake. Fortunately, he survived, suffering just some dizziness.

and a python had seemingly killed each other: the python having strangled the cobra, and the cobra having bitten the python.[37] I pondered how this might be read as an augury for the future or year ahead. The image constellated around the same time period as Steve's book. The year hadn't started out too well. In my journal for the 6th of January, 2018, based on watching a YouTube video clip, I had written about two dangerous clowns on the world stage: *"We begin with a nuclear scare. Kim Jong Un announcing a button (nuclear bombs) on his desk. Trump saying he has a bigger button on his desk and that his works! A precarious year ahead."*

In my journal, I noted that on Sunday, 11th of February, around the time of reading a part in Steve's book about Clint Eastwood as actor and then director, I had decided to go to a movie at our local cinema. It so happened that Eastwood's latest film, *The 15:17 to Paris*, was showing. It is a true story about a terrorist attack on a train, featuring the actual three US soldiers involved in this debacle as the actors. Of note is that the ISIS perpetrator on the train gets no airtime or any backstory. Steve's book explores this kind of issue, of empathetic (or lack of) engagement with the Other. His text also considers political hotspots such as a transforming Ireland (Northern Ireland and the Republic of Ireland), as well as Nelson Mandela during the transformational new South Africa. I felt his book was of value for our times, in bringing depth psychological concepts into the cultural arena.

PILGRIM DREAM

JOURNAL ENTRY, 2ND OF FEBRUARY 2018 (FRIDAY):

Dream of being on some kind of pilgrimage/journey (with a soul mate?). This is very much the road less travelled, characterised by a very rocky/ desert-like terrain. I pass a number of people. Mostly, they are in cars or trucks, along the way. The journey starts being uphill (mountain) with many twists and turns. After turning a corner, I find myself next to the sea. The tide is coming in. A vague fear of being washed into the dangerous waves. The part we are now negotiating is particularly steep. I notice, though, in a

---

[37] National Geographic, "King Cobra Reticulated Python Fight," February 5, 2019

way, it is a pilgrim path in that the rock ledges are quite smooth from use. I then arrive where there is doubt whether this is a path. It looks unrealistically challenging — at least for me, having a fear of heights. At this, I wake up.

A glaring life problem we faced as a family was financial difficulties. The prospect of not being able to afford our daughters' college costs would be tragic, especially in light of the high value we place on higher education. At college information evenings, I would often talk to parents, encouraging them about the golden opportunity a degree would provide. My upbeat persona was in stark contrast to an inner horror of the possibility of failing our own daughters, of not providing them with an educational opportunity. Reflecting on our financial situation, we could certainly blame the Irish economic fallout and being excluded from my father's will. However, Lyn and I, not being the sharpest tools in the shed, financially speaking, certainly added to the *folie á deux* of the situation.

The path ahead posed many dangers and possibly catastrophe. The next academic year, starting in September 2018, we would accept two cohorts for our Certificate in Jungian Psychology with Art Therapy. This was overtime income for me and also income for Lyn. With the economic pressure, there was a fire under us. The path we had chosen had its hazards and had got us into a desolate place. Though, as the sacred texts sometime say, it is in the desolate places that one might have an epiphany. Jungian psychology can be very insightful, to help along the path.

> … the unconscious always produces an impossible situation in order to force the individual to bring out his very best. Otherwise one stops short of ones best, one is not complete, one does not realize oneself. It needs an impossible situation where one has to renounce one's own will and one's own wit, and do nothing but wait and trust to the impersonal power of growth and development. [38]

For us, it was a case of becoming galvanized, in tandem with such good advice from the old man. In a state of grace,

---

[38] C. G. Jung, *Visions: Notes of the Seminar Given in 1930-1934* (London: Routledge, 1998), 321.

we would allow life itself to lend a helping hand. In many ways, we would follow our energy more in the way of the Fool rather than the considered way of the Magician. The High Priestess would also be making notable appearances.

Ishtar and Ophiuchus

Journal entry, 17th of March 2018 (Saturday): Paddies Day

I've been so busy the last while, and also on slow recovery from that flu/ cold. Slowly regaining strength but often feel eclipsed by financial circumstances, leaving me dizzy and drained.

About 3 days ago, I was invited by Dr. Thomas Arzt (co-editor of Jung's Red Book for Our Times *series, with Murray Stein) to contribute an article for the third volume of this series. He had just finished reading my Mercurius book, which he described as 'fascinating and enlightening'.*

This afternoon we have Dream Group.

Grace experienced a synchronicity recently. I had met her Thursday, three weeks ago at a café, to discuss her giving a talk at our upcoming Art and Psyche symposium with keynote Sylvia Brinton-Perera (giving a talk on the title of her notable book Descent to the Goddess). *The symposium was scheduled for Friday 13th of April.*

I chose the Ishtar clay tablet image from ancient Sumeria for the flyer. Her wings, clawed feet, and owls and cats by her ankles always appealed to me. I also found it quite an erotic image.

I had also discussed with Grace the importance of thirteen, especially as her birthday is on the 13th of October, and her progressed Sun entering this 13th sign a couple of years ago (Ophiuchus). This numerological aside seemed fitting for our upcoming event for the 13th of April.

So the synchronicity is that on the Sunday following our café chat, she was driving home back from Cork. As she drove past a Marian shrine (a bit before her turn-off), there was a guy parked there, with his pet owl. So she turned back to explore this more and chatted to the guy. The owl perched on her car mirror, so she took some pics.

I find this event fascinating, as it constellates a coniunctio of the dark powers (owl) with the powers of light (Mary) as if trying to reconfigure a new archetypal pattern: Mary and Ishtar.

This has correlations of meaning with the dream Grace shared. It included a scene of a mysterious young woman at her Slievenamon home, in which she finds herself in the ground in a kind of bath with this woman. We discussed this in terms of a ritual to reconnect with the chthonic.

The following day, I then mentioned in my journal about reading Erik Goodwyn's *Neurobiology of the Gods*, having ordered it for our college library. We had met Erik at the Jung in Ireland event in April 2017, in Galway, where we had a short discussion on the neurobiological basis of Jung's notion of the alchemical *coniunctio*.

JOURNAL ENTRY, 6TH OF MAY 2018 (SUNDAY):

On Friday the 13th of April [New Moon in Aries, Sun conjunct Moon] *we had our Approaching the Numinous art and psyche symposium. We had agreed to have Grace Wells, Peadar O'Callaghan, and Sylvia Brinton-Perera as keynotes.*

On the Tuesday before the event, we heard that Sylvia couldn't make it due to a snag at Jung in Ireland (Glenstal Abbey programme). We were kindly helped out. Erik Goodwyn was sent instead (we never knew he was even in the country, as he didn't appear in the brochure). It all worked out fine enough.

Strangely, I had recently completed reading his book. Lyn was busy reading it (and the book was due back in the library on the 13th of April — the very day of our symposium!).

This same Friday, the 13th, was the day my PhD student to be, Teresa Mason, requested a meeting with me to discuss PhD possibilities (this would end up being on Sheela-na-gig). It was the same day that there was a large arts activist march in Limerick that made national news, with our art college as a notable driver. This was in relation to the 8th amendment (to repeal current abortion laws).[39]

After our symposium in April, Lyn and I had a few days at the luxury five star Killarney Park hotel, having being invited again by the New York Centre of Jungian Studies, for another Jung in Ireland event. During this luxury experience, I wondered about the unusual circumstances we were in. What would our bank manager say about such extravagance? How disparate this all seemed! Life had certainly played us some unusual cards. The Fool was having fun.

---

[39] Emine Saner, "The Hateful Eighth: Artists at the Frontline of Ireland's Abortion Rights Battle," The Guardian, April 12, 2018.

A beautiful dream fragment in which my (anima/soul/world-soul) gives me the feeling of being her beloved.

Journal entry, 30ᵀᴴ of May, 2018 (Wednesday):

Finished working on my invited article/chapter for Jung's Red Book for our Times publication [titled Jung's Red Book and the Alchemical Coniunctio].

Got back home to add some finishing touches. Decided to check astrology and noticed Moon at 21 degrees Sagittarius. After incorporating some feedback from Lyn, I then emailed it off at 22 degrees Sagittarius. (Moon aligned with fixed star Ras Alhague).

My article was all about Sun (1913) and Moon (2014) in Ophiuchus, and with both events during a Full Moon. A synchronistic echo from history!

Dropped girls off at cinema 9PM then joined Lyn and friends for a drink at Carey's pub.

Walking to their table, I noticed some broken pieces of paper on the table just before arriving at 'our' table. Two joker cards had been torn into 4 pieces each (8 pieces in total).

Whilst researching for this article, I noticed that the first historiated initial in Jung's Red Book (*Liber Novus*) appearing after the frontispiece, includes a blue butterfly hovering amidst some flowers and foliage. This adventure, for Jung, was somewhat of a Fool's Journey following the impulses and wiles of psyche — an image of the *anima mundi*, the soul of the world. The first two paragraphs from this chapter:

On Friday, 12ᵗʰ of December, 1913, whilst at his desk deeply troubled, Jung took the decisive step to 'let himself go.' Sinking into a trance-like state, he entered an otherworldly imaginal realm that would remind him of the land of the dead. Thus began his so-called experiment as a confrontation with the unconscious. He chronicled the ensuing experiences, over the next few months, in what he called his *Black Books*. Over the following years, he developed commentary on the experiences, and artistically reworked the material into calligraphic text and exquisite images in the style of an illuminated manuscript. This became his *Red Book*, which he also titled *Liber Novus*.

Jung notes that the 12ᵗʰ of December was Advent. That evening, in 1913, the Moon was approaching a Full Moon in Gemini (Sun in Sagittarius). To be precise, it would be Full Moon the following night, on the 13th of December. This is noteworthy, as Jung at this stage of his life had already developed a keen interest in astrology. Less certain, though, was whether or not he knew that this portion of the sky, being traversed by the Sun, is also part of the 'serpent-bearer' constellation Ophiuchus (associated to the Greek Ascle-pius). This constellation has often been touted as the 13th sign as an alternative zodiac to the Aristotelian-derived 12 signs, prevalent in popular culture. The Sun during this time of the year was also moving into close conjunction (celestial longitude) with the brightest star in Ophiuchus, known as Ras Alhague. This star, on the forehead of Ophiuchus, as 'third eye', is associated in astrolog-ical lore with intuitive vision.[40]

Sheela-na-gig

Journal entry, 11th of August 2018 (Saturday): Solar Eclipse in Leo

We went on a Sheela-na-gig outing. About 15 of us met at a café in Fethard at 10AM, starting with a nice coffee. At 11AM, we departed for Kiltinan (about two miles from Fethard) to a farm where a castle is located next to a river. A small but very noticeable Sheela appears on the castle tower wall near the stream, from a nearby spring. It looks a bit like the horned god Cer-nunnos in lotus posture on the Gundestrup cauldron.

Then on to the derelict Chapel and graveyard at the exit of Kiltinan. At the corner, an occulted (placed sideways) Sheela. This work was stolen some years back — purportedly in the USA.

Returning to Fethard — on the town wall is the famed Witch on the Wall *(Pat, one of our guides, relayed a theory that it absorbed the angst of mothers in labour — like Christ suffering for our sins).*

A short stroll and around the corner, we then meet Sheela on the town wall. Had discussion of various theories. Liam, the character, full of opinions and colourful stories.

In all, we managed seven Sheelas, one Cat Goddess, and one stolen Sheela site during our outing. This was a big expe-rience, with far too much to write about. The Medieval village of Fethard has the highest concentration of Sheela-na-gigs in Ireland. The story of the stolen Kiltinan Sheela, originally on the small church wall at the top corner, and occulted (side-

---

40 Mathew Mather, "Jung's Red Book and the Alchemical Coniunctio," in *Jung's Red Book for Our Time: Searching for Soul under Postmodern Conditions, Volume 3,* ed. Murray Stein and Thomas Arzt (Asheville, NC: Chiron Publications, 2019), 255.

ways), had become an intrigue, with all sorts of fanciful theories about its abduction and current whereabouts. Sheela's charm certainly seems to have infiltrated the Fethard community and beyond. Perhaps she has transmitted a wry and heretical humour to the community, amongst other enigmatic qualities. Amongst our group on the day was Teresa Mason, my PhD student to be, specialising in Sheela-na-gig's transformative role for an Ireland in crisis and in transition.

THE CATHEDRAL AND THE FOOL

JOURNAL ENTRY, 21ST OF AUGUST, 2018 (TUESDAY):

Dreamed of being really good at being a contortionist, of getting out of tricky physical/body (twisted together) situations.

Over a coffee at a local café the day before this dream, my friend Sean handed me a slim, slightly tatty book, saying I could keep it as a gift. He had recently found it whilst busking with his tin whistle in Paris near Notre Dame. More precisely, it was chucked out of the nearby bookshop, Shakespeare and Company. No doubt, it was deemed unsellable, so they left it outside, knowing full well it would most probably end up in the garbage.

The book is titled *Utz*, by Bruce Chatwin. On its cover is a harlequin image of a character playing the flute. According to the publisher, this front cover is a photograph of The Fool from a Tarot deck made by Martin Boehme of Dresden around 1780. Having read it, Sean reckoned I would really appreciate it, as it featured one of my main interests: alchemy. I was intrigued, as around the time he found it, he was busking with a tin whistle, so there was a kind of mirror with the character on the book cover playing the flute. More intriguingly still, Sean had recently also completed writing his regular "Street Philosopher" column. It was titled "Instrumental in Iran: Sean Moran blows the whistle on Plato's flautophobia." All about the flute, the column features a black and white photograph of an old Iranian man playing this instrument.

I like such moments, as Sean veers toward rationalism and is sceptical about supposedly woo-woo subjects such as synchronicity, let alone alchemy, astrology, and magic! His second PhD is on 13th-century Thomas Aquinas's conception of the Christian Trinity, *sans* esoteric philosophy.

I was much more fascinated by this find than he was. As related earlier in this chapter, my PhD journey on Jung and Alchemy began in earnest on a day that I found a random Joker card outside our local Franciscan Friary in Clonmel. This was in 2005, almost exactly 13 years prior to Sean's find. My thesis on the alchemical Mercurius was very much about the divine jester (as previously mentioned, a character precluded from the Christian house of God). Now, some years later, the jester had reappeared outside a Cathedral. This time much more grandiosely — as an 18th century Tarot image of *The Fool* outside the Gothic cathedral of Notre Dame — and with a more elaborate message as the book *Utz*.

That evening, I read *Utz* in a single sitting, and realized I had seen the Hollywood film production a few years back. The film had made an enduring impression. Its alchemical themes are rather intriguing. I briefly distil some of them here, as they add a touch of the arcane to our journey.

The story is based on the gentleman Kaspar Joachim Utz in Prague, living through the Nazi invasion and then the Russian occupation until his death in 1974. Kaspar (Utz) had largely dedicated his life to collecting valuable Meissen porcelain figurines. This was a most precarious enterprise considering the fascist regime. His interest, though, began as a child before any foreign invasion. On a trip with his grandmother, he had become bewitched by a Harlequin antique porcelain figurine dressed in a costume of multi-coloured chevrons made by J. J. Kaendler, the greatest Meissen modeller.

It was only four years later, to console him over his father's death, that his grandmother bought him the figurine as a Christmas gift. As the author Bruce Chatwin describes;

> Kaspar pivoted the figurine in the flickering candlelight and ran his pudgy fingers, lovingly, over the glaze and brilliant enamels. He had found his vocation: he would devote his life to collecting —

"rescuing" as he came to call it — the porcelains of the Meissen factory.[41]

Inheriting his grandmother's estate made this possible. Porcelain, as it turns out, is partially an alchemical success story. Chatwin explains that by the seventeenth-century Chinese porcelain had begun to make an immense impact on the European imagination.

> [the Chinese] were thought to be very wise and to live to a very great age, dispensing arbitrary, impartial justice according to laws derived from Earth and Heaven. They drank from porcelain. They built pagodas of porcelain. The smooth and lustrous surface of porcelain corresponded to the smooth, unwrinkled surface of themselves. Porcelain was *their* material — as gold was the material of the Roi Soleil.[42]

Apparently, Kings and philosophers of the age loved the substance. The prominent seventeenth-century German mathematician and philosopher, Leibniz, "who had believed this world was the best of all possible worlds — believed that porcelain was its best material."[43]

The origin of porcelain, in the West, has been linked to the alchemist Johannes Böttger (1682 — 1792). As an early claim to fame, Böttger was reputed to have obtained a Red Tincture or Ruby Lion from a mendicant monk which could transmute lead into gold. After performing the operation amongst sceptical witnesses, his reputation spread. Unfortunately, though, he ended up being arrested and imprisoned in Dresden. Over the next thirteen years he was placed in the service of King Augustus the Strong and tasked to create the *arcanum universale* or Philosopher's Stone.

However, by 1706, the kingdom's resources were failing due to the exorbitant cost of the Swedish War and the King's obsessive purchases of Chinese porcelain. Böttger, still unsuccessful, was threatened with the torture chamber. Around this time, he met the talented chemist Tschirnhaus, a friend

---

[41] Bruce Chatwyn, *Utz* (London: Picador, 1989), 19.

[42] Ibid., 104.

[43] Ibid., 104.

of Leibniz, who was well on the way toward discovering the secret of making true porcelain. The sought-after requirement was a kiln capable of extremely high temperatures — as a "purgatorial hellfire" — of 1450 degrees centigrade, to fuse glaze and clay and thereby achieve, phoenix-like, a resurrection. Böttger, to save his skin, agreed to help Tschirnhaus.

They were successful. By 1708, he presented red porcelain to Augustus. This was followed, a year later, by white porcelain. In 1710, the Royal Saxon Porcelain Manufactury was established at Meissen. The chemical composition of the paste was referred to as the "arcanum" and was kept a state secret, though Böttger's assistant betrayed him by selling it to Vienna. Meanwhile, the Meissen factory thrived and indeed still exists today.

As Chatwin notes, though, the alchemist's gold was not the vulgar gold of charlatans, but rather a mystical technique to achieve spiritual transfiguration: "The search for gold and the search for porcelain had been facets of an identical quest: to find the substance of immortality."[44] Utz's figurines were "alive but not alive." They were a moment of 17th-century history immortalised by the breath of the alchemist or, in this case, the passionate attention of the collector, Utz.

Utz would take them out regularly and animate them with his operatic play amidst soft fluttering candlelight and grand music. In one excerpt, we read: "Columbine would be endlessly in love with Harlequin — 'absolutely mad to trust him.'"[45] A bit later, we read, "Harlequin ... the arch-improviser, the zany, trickster ... would forever strut in his variegated plumage ... dance in the teeth of catastrophe ... Mr Chameleon himself ."[46]

For the eighteenth-century imagination, porcelain, like gold, was more than a pretentious nicety of great monetary value. It was filled with talismanic magic imbuing the owner with qualities such as potency, invincibility, and longevity. It

44 Ibid., 109.

45 Ibid., 113.

46 Ibid., 114.

thus made sense why the King would fill his palace with about forty thousand items of porcelain.

As can be gathered, *Utz* was an intriguing read. It also arrived at an appropriate moment in my life. It not only resonated with my Fool theme but also helped to encourage my own efforts toward transmuting the lead of my life into something of greater value. Flecks of alchemical gold were certainly beginning to appear. Sean had arrived with the gift of a book and a story that reaffirmed a calling. It was re-enchanting and a reminder about how very fascinating alchemy can be, especially when affirmed so mysteriously by a synchronicity.

Over the next few days, still on summer vacation, I read about the Gothic Cathedral of Notre Dame. Sean, meanwhile, had returned for another busking trip to Paris. My rather superficial research soon dredged up the story of the enigmatic French alchemist Fulcanelli, whose book *Le Mystère Des Cathédrales* was published in 1926. In this work, he decodes much of the symbolism of Notre Dame, which can be read as a book in stone, at both exoteric and esoteric levels. At an obvious level, it portrays biblical iconography but also, according to Fulcanelli, depicts the secret of the Great Work.

Fulcanelli, whose identity has remained elusive, purportedly gave his assistant Eugène Canseliet a sample of projection powder. Canseliet apparently used this to perform a successful transmutation of lead into gold in the presence of reliable witnesses, Julien Champagne and Gaston Sauvage. Much intrigue, such as this, surrounds the life and work of Fulcanelli. There is no definitive birth or death date. Canseliet also refers not to his death, but to his *departure*. In alchemical lore, this implies someone who has succeeded in the Opus, and understandably requires the foil of having died.

Upon Sean's return from Paris, we met up again at the café, as I wanted to more fully explore the story of the card and the Cathedral and to clarify some of the timing. We agreed to meet on Sunday, the 26th of August, 2018, at 2:30PM, which happened to coincide with the Pope's grand public appearance in Ireland at Phoenix Park. The timing almost exactly coincided with a Full Moon in the ecclesiastical Pisces and the Sun in Our Lady Virgo.

Our rather abject café meeting contrasted with such a grand event, akin to a couple of jokers outside the officially endorsed sanctum of God. Astrologically speaking, this should not have been a surprise. The day Sean gave me the book coincided with the Sun transiting onto my ruling planet, Mercury, in Leo in my astrological chart. This is a signifier, par excellence, of alchemical gold-making. However, for this summer, my time was up. The academic year would be starting up at the beginning of September. More personal projects, such as this, would have to be shelved. To continue down this alchemical rabbit hole, at this time, would have been a dangerously foolish move.

BLUE BUTTERFLY

We now turn our attention, as does the Fool in some Tarot depictions, to the enchantment of a butterfly. 2018 was a busy year for me. It was only a week or so into December, after completing the bulk of academic chores, that I could finally start giving the blue butterfly article I was invited to write some proper attention.

The timing seemed apt. Our passageway through December, with its shortening days, corresponds to the mythic descent into the underworld and the enantiodromian turning point at solstice, out of the darkness. During this period, a couple of synchronistic phenomena on the theme of death and an afterlife stood out. The first was around December 8th and 9th, and the second was on December 15th.

Saturday afternoon, December 8th, was our monthly (more or less) dream group. One of our friends and dream group participants had brought a book for us titled *Proof of Heaven: A Neurosurgeon's Journey into the Afterlife,* by Dr. Eben Alexander.[47]

---

[47] This book loan was in response to mentioning news of a friend of ours who catastrophically experienced a seizure and fallen into a deep coma. He passed away some weeks later.

Apart from the title and story theme, what especially struck me was the image chosen for the cover: a blue butterfly.

Intrigued, I quickly devoured the book the following day, Sunday, the 9th. The story of Eben Alexander has an irony in that his job as a neurosurgeon often meant dealing with comatose patients and their families. He described himself as being firmly rooted in the scientific position of the day that debunks the afterlife as a wishful delusion. However, after his own brain was suddenly overcome with a rare illness, he ended up in a coma for seven days. His neocortex, responsible for consciousness, effectively shut down. It was considered a miracle when, against expectations of medical opinion, he revived and returned to a full recovery.

The real miracle, though, is described in the events that took place during his time in the coma, when there should have been no consciousness. He describes having experienced a lucid afterlife, meeting divine and loving beings, and profound revelations of the deeper mysteries of existence. A few excerpts as he moved through the gateway into the otherworld give a sense of this:

> I heard a living sound, like the richest, most complex, most beautiful piece of music you've ever heard … filaments of pure white light … tinged, here and there, with hints of gold … an opening … there was a whooshing sound, and in a flash I went through the opening and found myself in a completely new world. The strangest, most beautiful world I'd ever seen.[48]

In this otherworld, he then describes his feminine guide, his *anima:* "a beautiful girl with high cheekbones and deep blue eyes … we were riding along together on an intricately patterned surface, alive with indescribable and vivid colors — the wing of a butterfly. In fact, millions of butterflies were all around us."[49] Further on, we read "I saw the abundance of life

---

48 Eben Alexander, *Proof of Heaven: A Neurosurgeon's Journey into the Afterlife* (New York: Simon & Schuster, 2012), 38.

49 Ibid., 40.

throughout the countless universes, including some whose intelligence was advanced far beyond that of humanity."[50]

Reflecting on his experiences, he writes:

> I now have a greatly enlarged conception of what "vast" and "wonderful" really mean. The physical side of the universe is a speck of dust compared to the invisible and spiritual part. In my past view, spiritual wasn't a word that I would have employed during a scientific conversation. Now I believe it is a word that we cannot afford to leave out.[51]

Upon his recovery and return to everyday life, Dr. Eben Alexander has become an acolyte in the service of his otherworldly journey, with its far-reaching implications. It transformed his prior, deeply sceptical, worldview. Here we should remember that his is not an isolated case. There is a groundswell of similar accounts of near-death experiences (NDE), including Jung's.[52] In taking these seriously, we nudge ever closer toward a re-imagining and the possibility of a quantum leap for the human condition; a re-patterning of our culture from a caterpillar consciousness to a butterfly consciousness. Our very survival as a species, and much of the natural world, could depend on the successful navigation through this rite of passage.

The 15th of December, 2018, was our last teaching day for the semester; a full Saturday with our students on the Certificate in Jungian Psychology and Art Therapy, and my favourite topic: synchronicity. Lyn and I decided to work together for the full day (instead of taking turns during the day, as in the past). In the morning, students were requested to recount a synchronistic experience and to respond in word and image. After a group discussion, there was a short tea and coffee break. This was followed by a lecture up to lunchtime. After lunch, we then did a Web of Life workshop, similar to the day with Richard earlier in the year.

---

[50] Ibid., 48.

[51] Ibid., 82.

[52] See the *Visions* chapter in Jung's *Memories, Dreams, Reflections*.

One of our students had drawn a blue butterfly for the morning task, as this featured in what he considered a synchronistic experience. His recollection:

> My first sighting of the butterfly was in my grandmother's kitchen during her own wake. She had died maybe two days beforehand. At the time, she was lying in her coffin in the sitting room. It was the early hours of the morning, and the house was very quiet at the time, which is what drew me to the movement of the butterfly beside the window. It was maybe the next day in the afternoon while our extended family were sitting down to lunch that we saw a similar butterfly this time in the kitchen of my aunt (my grandmother's daughter). Her house is less than half a kilometre from my grandmother's house. I noticed the butterfly and commented that I had seen a similar butterfly the day before. I think it was my aunt that mentioned, in a very matter-of-fact manner, that it must be my deceased grandmother. I had never heard about this association until then. I recall that the first butterfly was blue, which was very striking considering it was then October and the days were getting darker. The second butterfly looked similar.[53]

Our student only recounted this story later in the day during the Web of Life workshop, as his randomly-selected object turned out to be a *butterfly*.[54] This was all especially notable, as butterflies, in folklore and mythologies around the world, are commonly associated with ancestral spirits. In addition, the butterfly symbolises major transitional life moments, such as a wedding and a death.[55]

We had run the Web of Life workshop a number of times, including at Killarney earlier in the year. On a number of occasions, the chosen object had activated the memory of a departed loved one or loved ones in a mysterious way, such as the example described above. It was as if this playful divinatory project, the Fool's Bag, was revealing itself, with one of its messages being to invoke the ancestral.

[53] Personal communication (email) dated December 30, 2018.

[54] A tortoise shell variety. Originally, we had included a ring with a piece of blue butterfly wing in the box but returned it to its owner (our friend Grace).

[55] Lyn recounts giving her grandmother a blue butterfly brooch for what turned out to be her last birthday.

Perhaps our over-intellectualised consciousness in mainstream academia has drifted too far into the confining box, drought, or malaise of rationalism, with a consequent loss of soul. In tracking the butterfly as muse, we open ourselves to the mystery of our being.

❧

There is a more problematic side of The Fool, as an eternal child *(puer* or *puella aeternus)*. His staff and bag are potential that remains in the realm of aspirational possibility. A carefree existence, without a worry in the world.

In our case, we were challenged, having our daughters to bring up and to *get real* and engage with the grittier responsibilities of life. Being more intuitive types, this meant moving our gaze from the clouds earthward to the practical realities of life. It would also drive us to unlock a deeper level of resourcefulness. Jung's illustrious collaborator, Marie-Louise von Franz, says it well:

> One of the most wicked destructive forces, psychologically speaking, is unused creative power ... if someone has a creative gift and out of laziness, or for some other reason, doesn't use it, the psychic energy turns to sheer poison. That's why we often diagnose neuroses and psychotic diseases as not-lived higher possibilities.[56]

In my diary on the last day of 2018, I reflected on my two cards of High Priestess and the Fool. I ponder if I have been chasing a butterfly over a cliff edge. I recall a dream from a couple of weeks prior in which we lived on the edge of a cliff, which I only realised when someone asked for directions. In responding, I noticed that down below it was green and lush.

This reminded me of a Zen story of the monk having accidentally fallen over the edge of a cliff. He was hanging on for dear life to a bush that was slowly dislodging, forced to confront an imminent fall to his doom. Yet, in this moment, he notices a beautiful flower nearby, and achieves enlightenment.

---

[56] Marie-Louise von Franz, *Shadow and Evil in Fairytales* (Dallas, Texas: Spring Publications, 1974), 177.

2019: STRENGTH (VIII)

Tracking the Butterfly; Green Lion; The Divine Feminine; African Queen; St John and the Vessel; Cancer Dei; Star Regulus; Sacred Marriage (and Brigid); Mantis

S trength, in the Rider-Waite Tarot deck: A refined woman in a white dress holding the head of a lion, in a gesture of gently subduing its dangerous nature. A wreath of foliage appears on her head, above which is a lemniscate. Around her waist is a belt of red flowers and greenery. In the far distance, on the viewer's left, is a mountain peak. It is number VIII in the Rider-Waite deck (XI in the Marseille deck).

Sallie Nichols describes the Strength card as the feminine soul within the male hero's unconscious: the anima, a figure who mediates between ego consciousness and the deeper realms of the unconscious as the instinctual animal soul. As her heart is pure, she has the inner strength to engage with wild powers without being harmed. She allows the hero to plumb the instinctive depths of psyche, to access its uncanny resilience and resourcefulness. This is not the hero macho-strength of a Samson or Hercules controlling the brutish, fearful symmetry of the lion, but rather a gentle and feminine approach toward engaging potent and dangerous libidinal forces. In Nichols' chapter on the Strength card, we read, "the acceptance of the animal soul is the condition for wholeness and a fully lived life."[57] In astrology, Leo is the royal sign ruled by the Lion. In depictions such as in Narnia, the lion is a regal, god-like being.

TRACKING THE BUTTERFLY

In my diary for the 1st of January, 2019, I noted having watched the Australian film *Walkabout* a couple of evenings ago (30th of December, 2018). I found this film fascinating but

---

[57] Jaffé, quoted in Nichols, *Jung and Tarot*, 213.

obviously also quite disturbing. Its opening montage holds a jaded mirror to our modern industrial and secular capitalist society: city life, workers, and consumer-culture. The story involves a desperate father who takes his teenage daughter and his younger son into the Australian outback in his black Volkswagen Beetle. Once there, he goes mad and starts to shoot at his children with a revolver. He misses, and they go scrambling deeper into the bush. He then places the revolver into his mouth and pulls the trigger in an act of suicide. The two children are then forced to find their way alone in the outback. They encounter a young Aboriginal man during his coming-of-age initiatory ordeal. They form a friendship, and, thanks to the Aboriginal youth's skills, they manage well. Two worlds and worldviews coincide: two traumatised Western children and the Aboriginal during his walkabout.

This story made for a conversation piece during our New Year's Eve party at our friends in their "heaven on earth" homestead, near the Knockmealdown mountains. Specifically, during a chat with my friend Michael Hickey, we discussed the film. Michael had lived in Australia during his coming-of-age years and ended up writing a book based on this, titled *Spuds in the Desert*. We share interests such as Jung, astrology, and writing, and so our conversations tend to veer into this area. Apart from the film, I also mentioned my Blue Butterfly story and the synchronistic phenomena it had constellated, as this was all fresh in my memory.

This reminded him of a remarkable recollection from his time in Alice Springs, Australia, during those formative years. His Aboriginal friend had requested that he dig a roughly six-foot-deep hole in the earth, which he promptly did. Some time later, his friend returned drunk with a knife and threatened to kill him. Around this moment, an exotic blue butterfly landed on the spade. Viewed as a synchronicity, there is a death-rebirth theme in this, considering his coming of age.

Went with Lyn to a café with the intention of drawing our yearly Tarot card. It was too busy and noisy, so we decided rather to do this at Saint Patrick's well as we needed to fetch water anyway.

Just after 12 (midday) whilst sitting on the small stone bridge at the well. A lovely day, with sunshine, and murmuring of the water, stillness. Cleared clutter of thoughts, collected major arcana, shuffled, and then I drew first — The Fool! 0 (thought I was done with him, lol). I decide to draw a second card — Strength VIII.

Lyn pulled Justice XI.

On the 3rd of January, I noted in my journal a coffee shop conversation with a South African friend. He recounted a story of his childhood when a schoolmate got killed whilst chasing a butterfly over a waterfall. He was only 16 or 17 years old.

The Fool could be viewed as "civilized man" in rebellion — as a return to nature. In depictions of him featuring a butterfly, he is carefree, tracking the ephemeral enchantments of life, and following a calling into nature — the whisperings of his indigenous soul. Yet having his "head in the clouds" could also lead to danger on the ground. There is a little dog at his feet that seems to be warning him of an impending danger. The dog is trying to get the Fool's attention, to look closer to earth and at the danger close at hand (the cliff). In Jungian psychology, we might say the sensation function required some attention.

GREEN LION

The Lion in the Strength card is a personal symbol, since I am a Leo in astrology. It is a reminder of the importance of reconnecting to one's animal soul, not in a brutal, subduing, and heroic way, but rather via the gentle and soft touch of the inner feminine. It is the anima as psychopomp and mediator of transpersonal powers.[58] This symbol also reminded me of one of Jung's Bollingen stone engravings, the anima milking

---

[58] My progressed Sun moving from Virgo (earth) entering Libra (air) would also conjunct my natal Mars this year. Sun conjunct Mars in Libra (ruled by Venus) fits the symbolism of the Strength card, especially considering my natal Sun being in Leo.

Pegasus. The inner feminine, as anima, mediating a "supernatural food" as libido from the transpersonal.

In my journal entry for the 2nd of February, I note extreme weather events around the world, possibly the coldest on record. Freezing temperatures in some States of the USA. Then, a heatwave in Australia, with temperatures above 40 degrees Celsius. In South Africa, after longstanding droughts, there is a severe water crisis. I also noted my first experience of being in an electric car. A distinct impression emerges that we are rapidly entering a new era.

Over a month later, in my journal, I noted that on Thursday evening, the 14th March, we had our Red Book Reading Group evening. We read and discussed chapter XIII, "The Sacrificial Murder." This section features one of the goriest scenes in the Red Book. In the imaginal landscape, Jung finds himself in a disturbing valley with red serpents "oozing." He comes across a young girl with brains splattered in a gruesome scene. Jung is instructed by a nearby priestess to reach into the child's body and break a piece of her liver off and to eat it. After plucking up the courage to eventually do this, the priestess nearby then lifts her veil. It turns out she is the girls' soul.

We remarked how the girl could symbolise the state of the soul of the Western world, being mutilated, desecrated, and murdered by a toxic patriarchy over the past centuries. Being instructed to eat a piece of her liver by the priestess could be viewed in terms of a mass, akin to the Catholic ritual. However, in this case, the mass is for the earthly and common soul of the world, rather than a transcendent Jesus in heaven. The liver, as Jung points out in *Memories, Dreams, Reflections*, was viewed in earlier times as the seat of the soul, in that it has the capacity to regenerate itself. Considered as a mass, Jung's life task could be viewed as being in the service of this soul of the world, to embody it, and to enact it through his life and works.

We also discussed the child prodigy, Greta Thunberg, a prominent climate change activist. In this year she was 16 years old and would inspire mass climate demonstrations across the globe.[59] Apart from huge support, she has suffered much abuse. To quote:

> … politicians … ridicule us on social media, and have named and shamed me so that people tell me that I'm retarded, a bitch and a terrorist, and many other things …I am just a messenger, and yet I get all this hate.[60]

The next day, Friday the 15th of March, in Limerick, I was contemplating this image whilst thinking about my alchemy preparation scheduled for the following day, Saturday. Whilst driving, after having lunch in town, waking images came to me of this as a mass. However, instead of the liver, I found myself eating a piece of a lion's heart, in light, especially, of my Tarot card Strength for the year. This was a mass to integrate the animal soul and to find my own strength. The woman in my Strength card I related to my *anima*, including her as a personification of the *soul of the world*, as a kind of priestess.

A bit earlier, after my lunch in Limerick, I bumped into a large school children's protest for climate action parading through the streets.[61] Upon returning to work at around 2PM, I had about half an hour to spare before fetching our daughter from the University of Limerick. In this short space of time, I decided to watch a video on Adam McLean's impressive alchemy website. A few minutes in, there was an image of the Tarot card Strength (from the Alchemy Tarot deck). It features a woman riding a large male Green Lion. She is wearing a loose-fitting white dress reminiscent of Renaissance statues of classical goddesses and muses. Her right breast is erotically exposed. With her right hand, she holds a flaming heart-cup into which pour a Sun liquid and a Moon liquid.

---

[59] In this year, 2019, she would be chosen as TIME magazine person of the year, and have a book published *Greta Thunberg: no one is too small to make a difference* (on the New York Times bestseller list).

[60] Greta Thunberg, *No One Is Too Small To Make A Difference* (Harlow, England: Penguin Books, 2029), 21.

[61] This day would see around 1.5 million protestors across the globe from about 125 countries, inspired by Greta Thunberg's climate activism.

This was a notable synchronicity in that it appeared shortly after my active imagination involving a Lion's heart and a contemplation of the Strength card. She holds up a grail-like vessel that contains a *coniunctio* (conjunction) of the opposites of Solar-masculine and Lunar-feminine, to be united through the feeling function of the heart.

On the way to Limerick that morning, we listened on the car radio about an extremist right-wing Australian 28-year-old who assaulted a Mosque in Christchurch, New Zealand, killing fifty-one people. In pondering this tragedy, I contemplate distilling out the Sun as a symbol of Christianity and the Moon as a symbol of Islam, and invite a personal mass of the heart to integrate the living waters of both religions.

THE DIVINE FEMININE

24TH OF MARCH JOURNAL EXCERPT:

On the evening of the Full Moon[62] this last week, I came across, on social media, this huge arts installation of a Moon inside St. Mary's Cathedral in Limerick.[63]

This week saw the completion (almost) of planning for our Divine Feminine event, also taking place in a church turned art gallery in LSAD (Limerick School of Art and Design). We added a 4th woman, Nóirín ní Riain, to begin with her Ode to Bridget.

I've been contemplating a lot on the alchemical image of Strength. It has become my symbol contemplating how libido can flow as Logos (Father) and Mythos (Mother), to give strength as a continuous Holy Communion to address loss of soul, and loss of psychic energy.

On this Super Full Moon, we also submitted documentation to the academic council for a special purpose award pilot module titled Art, Psyche and the Creative Imagination.[64] This would later develop into an MA.

---

[62] This was also a super Full Moon, coinciding with spring Equinox. Moon in Virgo — transiting into Libra, Sun in Pisces — transiting into Aries.

[63] Art installation by Luke Jerram.

[64] Apart from a super Full Moon at spring Equinox, the planet Jupiter was also at 23 degrees Sagittarius, which aligns in celestial longitude to fixed star Ras Alhague ('third eye' of the constellation Ophiuchus/Asclepius).

In my journal for the 14th of April, I recount recent experiences in Enniskillen in Northern Ireland, where Lyn and I had the good fortune of a few days at a luxury hotel for the annual Jung in Ireland study seminar on the topic of Facing Mortality: Fear of the Unknown. The two workshops we delivered (twice each) were titled Spirals of Life, Brushes with Death, and Re-membering: Threads of Golden and Silver Light.

During our free day, we went for an outing to the Marble Arches Geopark Caves. The memorable part of this was a tour into the "womb of the earth," where we witnessed a range of crystalline marvels with fanciful names such as: a church organ, guardian angel, underwater Atlantis, a fossilized star fish, and much more.

Upon our return and after lunch, Lyn and I went for a walk to the nearby riverside. During our return, strolling up the outside wooden stairs, I came across a blue beetle crossing my path. A few moments later, a second one, and then, right in front of me, was a third beetle. This one was dead, so I picked it up and have it as one of our natural objects we use for our web of life workshops.

This event had significant synchronistic meaning for me, considering Jung's scarab beetle incident and all the associated Egyptian mythological amplifications on the theme of the heart and around death and rebirth. I understood it in terms of a death of my current persona and a rebirth into a mode more aligned to the project on our horizon as the Art, Psyche and the Creative Imagination programme. Psyche is sometimes depicted as a butterfly, that quintessential symbol of a transformation mystery from caterpillar to winged creature. Similarly, the beetle (such as a scarab or my blue beetle) undergoes a transformation. In essence, this cave and beetle experience was symbolically akin to a return to the archetypal mother (cave) to be reborn into a new state of consciousness, lighter and with a sense of greater spaciousness.[65] This experience coincided with springtime and moving toward Easter.

---

[65] This Blue Beetle synchronicity is a separate essay.

My journal entry for the 14th of April ends with a few remarks about our upcoming two-week holiday and our Art and Psyche symposium on the Divine Feminine. My nephew, Jack, with a heart of gold and with dreadlocks and all, would be visiting from Australia. Our oldest daughter's 21st birthday was on the 9th of April. A couple of friends our daughters' age were also down from New Zealand, all of them looking after our home and our cat whilst we were away.

On the 15th of April, Notre Dame Cathedral in Paris burned down. The following day, the third holiest Islamic site, the Al Aqsa Mosque in Jerusalem, was on fire, though this was much less serious.

24TH OF APRIL JOURNAL EXCERPT:

On Sunday morning [21st of April] Jack started the day noting a snail climbing up the wall and then a small red spider, as well.

Later in the morning, whilst driving to find a coffee shop, he noticed a small spider and web on the dashboard of the car. This precipitated my elaboration on the spider from a symbolic point of view and its connections to synchronicity.

(Moon transiting in Scorpio) Then, after parking at the Dove Hill restaurant, I spied a silver object at my foot. It turned out to be a silver spider brooch with one red eye (other fallen out).

In my lectures on synchronicity, I would often begin with a spider story from when I was 17 or 18 years old. I was at the end of a weekend pass from my military conscription (two years in the Air Force as a dog handler), and that Sunday afternoon, I reluctantly asked my mother to drop me at the bus station to return to camp. As we walked down the stairs from the kitchen to the outside garden, I felt a slight resistance on my head. I then noticed it was a strand of spider web from a nearby tree and, furthermore, noticed a large spider hurtling along toward me. In a panic, my mother helped me untangle and break free from the impending danger. I remember her remarking, "there's doctor Jung at work again" (a phrase she would often use whenever we encountered a synchronicity).

I had found her comment unusual. I did not recognise any synchronicity at the time. Years later, though, it began to make sense. Being caught in the invisible threads of a spider's web can be symbolic of being ensnared in a negative mother complex. The spider, who spins a web into creation, but who can then imbibe it back into her being, is also symbolic of the Great Mother archetype capable of creative and destructive rhythms. The spider, as spinner, can also connote the creative instinct. In mythology, for instance, one might reflect on the three fates, spinners of past, present, and future.

In that moment, though, it was more the positive mother complex that gave my mother the good sense of helping to release me "into the world." She also had the wisdom to recognise this as a synchronicity. Jung would say that synchronistic phenomena can constellate around a particular archetype — in this case, certainly, the Great Mother but also that of Hero archetype, a young lad who needed to engage with the world, leave his mother's house, and return to the initiatory *realm of the fathers.* In relation to the card Strength, this is the aspect of the feminine helping to mediate archetypal powers. Perhaps recounting the story to my nephew Jack also had some magic in it. He was in a new land and on the cusp of planning his next steps into Europe. A story such as this was about the best I, as his uncle, could muster.

Our 4th annual Art and Psyche symposium on The Divine Feminine was scheduled for Friday, the 26th of April. I would later understand the symbolism of the spider as a compensatory symbol, in that it included not only the creative instinct but also more destructive and negative polarities of our topic. The accompanying exhibition and keynote talks veered more toward the so-called positive aspects of the Divine Feminine.

28TH OF APRIL JOURNAL EXCERPT:

After lunch, on Thursday, Lyn and I went to fetch Veronica Goodchild at the airport.

It was lovely to meet her. We had an immediate soul connection. We then went back to the Absolute Hotel to check us all in and meet with our other presenter, Mary Condren, for dinner (five of us — Lyn, Jack, Mary Condren, Veronica, and myself). A notable memory is that Mary told us about her synchronistic experience of finding a piece of bog wood whilst collecting blackberries. It was a natural sculpture of a serpent and an Earth Goddess.[66]

The next morning was the largest symposium we've had so far, with over a hundred of us. Nóirín Ní Riain[67] *opened with sacred song. This was followed by Mary Condren talking on Brigit and 21st century Ireland, during which she elaborated two myths: of Patrick as sacrifice and Brigit as mercy.*

After the break, Veronica Goodchild presented on Dreams, Synchronicity, and Pilgrimage in her bare feet. The morning ended with Marian Dunlea on Anima Mundi.

After lunch, there were 4 parallel workshops. I was in Veronica's workshop on shamanic journeying to a drum.

We then ended the day with us all coming together and Nóirín enticing us into a snake dance. Storm Hannah (red weather alert in Clare) moved in that evening.

We were very happy with the event, which was held in the church gallery.

This symposium on The Divine Feminine was a living illustration, for me, of a new feminine strength gaining momentum within our cultural arena. The following morning, a Saturday, the news mentioned that Storm Hannah had knocked out the electricity supply for about twenty-one thousand homes across Ireland. However, in Limerick at the Absolute Hotel, it was a beautiful morning. Over breakfast, we met with Veronica. We noted the Sun streaming into the restaurant space, glistening on the river below. Two swans were paddling along amidst the shimmering sunlight. It was like an impressionist painting.

We had a day planned with Veronica. We started at the Milk Market to get a few picnic goodies. This included my favourite luxuries from a Turkish vendor — authentic baklava and a freshly squeezed orange and pomegranate juice. Our day outing was to the myth-rich Lough Gur, and then to a Grange stone circle nearby.

A further excerpt from my journal:

Whilst at Lough Gur, and just before reaching the top point of the walk, I found a silver Xmas bauble tree decoration with the words Ho, Ho, Ho writ-

---

[66] Mary Condren is author of *The Serpent and the Goddess: Women, Religion and Power in Celtic Ireland* (1989), and is a scholar at Trinity College Dublin with a particular interest in Brigit.

[67] Dr Nóirín Ní Riain is a notable Irish musical performer, and an ordained Minister.

ten on it. I wondered if this could be a kind of Hermes As-Above, So-Below moment? Silver as Lunar — feminine. The Lake, with its mythology of a Goddess living in its depths, wearing a green cloak.

Toward the end, Veronica accidentally activated voice number 12 (on our audio guides). It mentioned swans as we were walking along the lakeside with a couple of swans paddling. It was as if this water plus two swans had constellated as a story theme for the day (considering the 2 swans at breakfast). Also, at the highest point, I had seen a bunch of bees on the stone wall, with copulation moments taking place. These couple-ships, no doubt enlivened by springtime, spoke the obvious. I pondered on the possibility of our next symposium theme as the Sacred Marriage.

On Thursday, the 16th of May, we got our Art, Psyche and the Creative Imagination short course approved, a couple of days prior to the Flower Full Moon (Sun in Taurus, Moon in Scorpio). On Friday, the 17th of May, we had an Art and Psyche morning, Awakening the Soul, followed by a Q&A on our courses after lunch. Good interest in our work.

15TH OF JUNE JOURNAL EXCERPT:

About a week ago, I dreamt that Veronica Goodchild's book Songlines of the Soul was a "bird" and one of a flock of birds, and that I should get to know this flock of birds. This was most vital and would teach me dragon language, the language of the earth.

AFRICAN QUEEN

I decided to visit South Africa to celebrate my mother's 80th birthday. This was also a rare opportunity to meet up with my brother (living in Australia) and my sister (living in Natal, South Africa). The flight I managed to book included a few hours' stopover at Frankfurt in Germany, scheduled for close to summer solstice, the 20th of June.

This date is notable considering my strength card, as the Lion is associated with St. John the Baptist (wearing a Lion skin, living in the wilderness, uttering prophetic cries akin to the roar of a Lion). Summer solstice is associated to John the Baptist, just as Christ's day is close to the winter solstice. The summer solstice coincides with the transition of the Sun from the air sign of Gemini into the water sign of Cancer. It fits the symbolism of being baptised. Summer solstice is the mid-year Sun, the longest day of the year, and so has a symbolic correlation to mid-day in the smaller time cycle of a day. We did our Tarot reading on the 1st of January, close to mid-day, and at Saint Patrick's well, where our well-keeper might be considered a "bush Baptist."

Whilst in Frankfurt, I decided to visit the Stádel Museum, which houses a large collection of historical artworks. One that stood out for me was a 15th-century depiction of St. Jerome and the Lion, by Master of the Housebook (1480). The image depicts a compassionate and pious Saint Jerome in white and red robes and with a halo. His hat includes the shape of a lemniscate, as we see in the Strength card (and the Magician card) in the Rider-Waite deck.

He is holding a thorn plucked out of the Lion's paw. The well-groomed and well-fed Lion is sitting at his side like a pet dog, sporting a rather strange expression. The story goes that during one of his lectures, a Lion with a thorn in his paw appeared. After plucking it out, the Lion was forever thankful and became his pet or familiar. St. Jerome apparently lived a lascivious life in Rome prior to his conversion to a life of Christian virtue. Patron saint of students, amongst other things, he encouraged a life of celibacy and purity. He is especially renowned for his female followers.

This painting added further nuance to my Strength card. St. Jerome, pious as he was, had an earlier, wilder life enjoying hedonic pleasures. His mythologised image — having compassion for wilder instincts — reframes the more brutal monster-slaying hero motif. He embodies a virginal-like purity and innocence, and thereby has a kinship with the natural potencies we see in Virgin and Beast motifs, such as the Virgin in the forest with a Unicorn sleeping in her lap. According to Jung, wild elemental natural-mythic forces, such as a Unicorn or the winged Pegasus, are symbols of the Holy Ghost. This can be interpreted as the presence of the divine numinous manifested through the innocence and purity of the virgin. Virgin, here, can be interpreted psychologically as a state of an inward-oriented consciousness receptive to transpersonal energies, and untainted by an extroverted secular worldliness.

The flight to South Africa reminded me of an enantiodromian swing, as represented in the Yin-Yang symbol. In the heart of Yang (summer), the dark Yin (winter) principle is born. Here, on the summer solstice, I was leaving summer behind to enter the Southern hemisphere and the heart of winter. I had planned to fall asleep on the flight as soon as possible, with the help of a drink or two.

The idea of chatting to a stranger sitting next to me held no appeal. However, as fate would have it, I ended up next to this guy who lives in the suburb of Muizenberg, where I lived for some months whilst a student in Cape Town. It turned out we shared many interests, including Jung, wilderness, and sustainability. We must have chatted for about six hours without interruption. His wife, next to him, was the creative director of an animation studio. At this stage of my career, I was co-director of the Bachelor of Science (Honours) in Digital Animation Production. Who would have thought of the strange symmetries! This was a welcome *anam cara* (soul friend) in the liminal passage en route to Cape Town, South Africa.

I have always found Cape Town (likened to the San Francisco of Africa) to be a dynamic and edgy city. Creativity and a spiritual energy permeate it, despite its many problems. Whilst there, for instance, a Sunday newspaper headline reads "World's most Dangerous City" citing a suspected twelve hundred and eighty murders in the first four months of the year.

During my stay, I took the Southern Suburbs Metro. In part, this was due to a miscalculation in which I missed my bus to Grahamstown/Makhanda, and in part, it was perhaps a slip-up allowing for a nostalgic remembrance from my student days as a regular commuter to Muizenberg. These were colourful days that included many a dubious happening. A fairly regular feature on this commute, for instance, would be an evangelist proselytizing with prophetic warnings and hopeful promises if you "give your life to Jesus."

Walking to the train, in the platform shadows, my first impression of the initial carriage was not so great. It had this black graffiti, making it feel like a death train. There was something ominous and not so cool about it.

Hardly anyone was on the train. There was a soulful and nostalgic feel to the day. The seat in front of me was ripped, and swear word graffiti sprayed on the walls. Sticker adverts on the carriage walls are fairly numerous. One of them reads: Dr. Chubi bring back lost lover. Stop love from cheating. Penis enlargement 4 hours. Money in account 5 hrs. [phone number]. Another one reads: Mama Hope: Financial problems, Magic stick and wallet, Lost Lover [phone number]

Between Cape Town station and my station, Diep River, there were three unplanned delays of about 15-20 minutes each. The woman across from me phoned to "give out" to whoever at the Metro. This was all amidst someone else playing African Queen music too loudly. A couple of French girls (perhaps in their early twenties) were on the train with us.

During the train trip, we passed this huge graffiti of a horned character, as if emerging from below the earth, in black and white and with "free Radovan" (a gang lord in prison). The next day, I come across his story in a news feed.

Eventually, after the train, I got back to [my friend] with the kind help of a middle-aged woman who stopped to give me a lift.

If the summer solstice is associated with a baptism, then my experiences back into South African culture afforded a range of baptismal emotions in the now established post-apartheid New South Africa. On the ground, I was heartened by the many random acts of kindness that cut across racial divides. The following day, I would catch the right bus, from Cape Town to Makhanda/Grahamstown.

After a challenging bus journey with its television station espousing endless evangelical films and promotion of their business, I arrived, albeit some hours late, in Grahamstown/Makhanda and met up with my mother, brother, and sister. The last time the four of us were together must have been over fifteen years ago.

On the first night of being at my mother's (25th of June), I had a short but notable dream: *Facing the sea, I take this stupendous dive, surprising myself at the spectacle, into the sea. A marvellous feeling.*

Pondering the dream, I was reminded of an excerpt from an analysis of the animated film *The Lion King*, in which it is described how a sports star can outperform their best performance at a moment of pressure, as can happen at an important competition. My interpretation was that the sea represented "archetypal Great Mother" and that a return to my literal mother resonated with Great Mother as a life journey, including trying to impress her. It felt as if my life was finally getting to the point of being as impressive as it realistically could be!

ST. JOHN AND THE VESSEL

JOURNAL EXCERPT 30TH OF JULY: MOON IN CANCER, APPROACHING SUN IN LEO (NEW MOON ON 1ST OF AUGUST)

Dream fragment — there were these silver objects (like a charm bracelet) at the bottom of a pot. I was lifting some of them out using a kind of chopsticks or tweezer/tongs. After a few of these varied shapes (Eiffel tower ...) are lifted out, I then place them in a cup. An instruction is given that one must mix in orange juice and then drink it. This is quite an original drink. The silver objects were some kind of edible foodstuff, though there was also a sense of more silver objects in the pot that were paper, and not really edible.

This dream got me reflecting on the alchemical Tarot Strength card that features a flaming heart cup into which pour the Sun and Moon liquids for a holy communion. It occurred when the Moon was in Cancer (Moon rulership) and the Sun in Leo (Sun rulership), and so was a very apt and timely symbol, and a visceral reminder about the integration of so-called anima/animus opposites, of "supernatural," transpersonal energies. An association with the silver objects was my mother's silver charm bracelet with a heart-shaped clasp. Amongst the objects on it were a Sun and a Moon.[68]

A couple of days later, Lyn and I headed west to stay over at our friend's in Ventry, in County Kerry. I often mention this area, as far west as you can go, as my spiritual home. We left on my birthday, the 1st of August, for a mini holiday for two

---

[68] My mother is Sun-sign Cancer, and I am Sun-sign Leo.

nights. I only caught up on my journal upon our return to Clonmel.

At Lucy's, I made a lovely sea bass dinner, accompanied by some white wine.

After dinner in the lounge, amidst a cosy old-fashioned fire, Lucy told us about her MA dissertation on the Clay Pot, and how it related to her art project of collecting a piece of clay from every county in Ireland. She made a small pot for each county and then created four larger vessels – one for each province — Leinster, Munster, Ulster, and Connacht. After this, she created a single and final large pot for all the counties on the island of Ireland. Not having a kiln meant she was dependent on other potters in the area, which was tricky regarding timing.

The final large pot ended up getting fired on the recent summer Solstice. However, tragedy struck. Upon lifting it up from the kiln, it slipped through her fingers and crashed into pieces.

Some time later, after recovering from the initial devastation, she made another large pot.[69] We had the pleasure of now witnessing its alluring simplicity and appealing aesthetic. I playfully and ritualistically placed my head in it as a kind of baptism into a one Ireland. Lyn also did this.

My associations were also to the grail vessel, which includes a mythos around St John (St John's Day coincides with the summer solstice). The mystery has a chain of associations that include: grail — baptism — St John — Merlin — Eagle.[70]

The next day, Lucy took us to a sacred site that included an oratorium (a small stone enclave) and the gravestone of Saint Manchan, which included a roughly hewn Celtic Cross. The surroundings are a spectacular natural amphitheater, giving a sense of vastness, including a 360-degree view onto the vault of the heavens. In the distance, on the sealine, is a view of the M-shaped Skellig Michael islands.

After our jaunt here, and before driving back, Lucy popped in to see the local farmer. We were invited into his home with an enthusiastic welcome also by his friendly sheep dog. Before long, we were sampling his various bottles of poteen[71], distilled using the nearby holy Well water. On St John's Day every

---

[69] At a later stage she also repaired the original one, kintsugi style.

[70] The subject of a separate story I wrote titled *As Far West As You Can Go*.

[71] Poteen, derived from the Irish word *pot*, has also been known as "Moonshine," and "Mountain Dew." It is typically distilled from ingredients that include potatoes or cereals and tends to have a high alcoholic content of between 40 to 90% by volume.

year, he officiates a small event, including poteen, for some of the local community.

I noticed on one of his home-made labels an image of white lightning coming out of a black bird's mouth. This seemed apt. Looking at the landscape after these shots was intense, a sense of spiritual edginess.

All of this coincided with the Leo New Moon (Sun conjunct Moon).

CANCER DEI

On the second day of this mini two-day holiday, Lucy had booked us into a seaweed spa treatment near Ballyferriter on the seashore. This ended up as quite the sensual experience, each being in a hot bath filled with nutrient-rich slime embracing our naked bodies, akin to an intra-uterine experience with water and placenta. After about half an hour in the bath, we went for the recommended dip in the sea. Lyn went ahead but ended up slipping and falling quite hard on her bum. I then followed and went about waist-deep into the cold water. Below me in the water, I spied something round, and so I dunked in to collect it. It was a large, intact but dead crab about the size of my head. I sensed this was my found object of the trip.

It was only whilst driving back that I realized a chain of correspondences: Crab — Cancer — solstice — John the Baptist. It was as if a baptism experience was awaiting us here in Ventry, even if it was over a month after the summer solstice.

In terms of the actual constellations, the Sun traverses the fixed stars in the constellation Cancer the crab every year around the time of my birthday, as was currently taking place. So this birth-like experience of being in a slimy warm bath, and then exiting into a cold outside big world, has echoes to a literal birth experience taking place during the Sun's passage through the crab constellation. Finding a crab in the seawater as an As Above, So Below moment was symbolically enervating — a synchronicity.

We had agreed to meet Lucy at the Ventry pottery and coffee shop as an *au revoir,* before departing back home. I noticed a range of about five or six large Celtic ceramic designs, a meter or so in diameter, in the shop. Nearby was a book of the various ceramic designs. I opened it to find a crab sculpture as a *Céade Mile Fáilte.*[72] Lucy then told us the crab sculpture itself had sold an hour or so earlier. All of this emerged over a coffee and cake at about midday.

We then left via Dingle, where we popped into one of our favourite restaurants. Whilst in Dingle, I wanted to visit the local bookshop to buy myself a birthday gift. I was very happy to find my next John Moriarty book, titled *Invoking Ireland.* I consider Moriarty's work to be visionary and even prophetic of an Ireland in transition.

Back home, I found *Invoking Ireland* so intriguing that I almost completed it in a day. As prophet John Moriarty invokes a bird reign and a return to the values of the Tuatha Dé Dannan. He describes the Tuatha Dé as magic makers in accord with nature, as opposed to the more wilful Fomorians, whose nature-controlling values have largely shaped the Irish way of life today. In this text, he also writes of star constellations and suggests not only an *Agnus Dei* (lamb of God) but also a *Cancer Dei* (crab of God). For him, the sacred Skellig Islands are an earthly crab-claw mirror to the celestial constellation.

STAR REGULUS[73]

The 23rd of August, when the Sun conjuncts Star Regulus after transitioning from Leo into Virgo, was the birthday of my father, who passed away in 2014. He was born when the Sun was in conjunction with Star Regulus, heart of the Lion. His larger-than-life personality fit, in many ways, this configuration. The heart, as symbol, was also of especial significance in that he was part of the team of doctors with the fa-

---

[72] Irish for "a hundred thousand welcomes," often used as an Irish welcome in their home.

[73] Star Regulus, known as one of royal stars of Persia, is the brightest star on the ecliptic. In the constellation Leo, it is the heart of the Lion. Every year around the 22nd or 23rd of August the Sun transits it, with the transition from Leo to Virgo. This star is also considered, in some astrological circles, as the marker of precession. In 2012 it precessed from Leo into Virgo. It stays in Virgo for the duration of a Platonic month of ~2160 years. Arguably, the Age of Aquarius coincides within this timeframe.

mous Chris Barnard, who performed the first heart transplant.

A heart attack, followed some months later by a stroke, would be the death blows sending my father into the mysterious beyond. Every year on the 23rd of August, on his birthday, I have a quiet remembrance of his life.

JOURNAL EXCERPT 24TH OF AUGUST: ZEN MASTER DREAM (DREAM ON THE NIGHT OF THE 23RD OF AUGUST)

I dreamed of a few of us meeting this Zen Master in a field of wheat. It is known that fire erupts spontaneously in this field from time to time, but that it isn't radically damaging — as if it is always contained in itself, and is quite small.

I find myself with some others, including Lyn, and we see one of these fires — it is circular, about 2-3 metres in diameter, but then dies down, as they do. Then the Zen Master is in front of us and talks to us about love.

A wheat field is a symbol associated with Virgo. She holds a sheaf of wheat in her hand (the star Spica), associated with the mystery of rebirth and of the harvest. A spontaneous circular earth-fire can be amplified with the notion of the alchemical *Lumen Naturae* (Light of Nature). Such a light of nature in a wheat field fits the symbolism of Star Regulus in Virgo. The heart of the Lion as an earth light, a kind of bubble, emerging from the heat of the earth's core as the summer begins to reach closure. The Zen Master, perhaps, was a personified expression of the wisdom of the earth, posing questions of the heart.

Around this time, I was reading Henry Corbin's heretofore unpublished writings in a book collection titled *Jung, Buddhism and the Incarnation of Sophia*, published earlier in the year. The dream seemed to embody the essence of some of these writings. The heart, as the "organ of the imagination," would be key to our Art, Psyche and the Creative Imagination project.

SACRED MARRIAGE (AND BRIGID)

JOURNAL EXCERPT 4TH OF SEPTEMBER:

Last Friday, the 30th of August, Lyn and I went to visit Grace at Ennistymon and stayed over for the night. Grace has a lovely place nestled in the woods next to a river and only a few minutes walk from the town centre.

That evening, we went to dinner at The Little Fox. I had a tasty lamb chop curry, followed by a dessert. Our stay coincided with a New Moon in Virgo (Sun conjunct Moon).

On Saturday, we visited the beach, which included a visit to the sixth-century Saint McCreevy chapel right on the seashore, where he purportedly fought off an eel/otter monster stealing bones from the graveyard. After an exhilarating beach walk with hound Mani careering around, we went to visit Brigid's Well, a bit further up on the hill. It is rather dramatic, and includes a passage into where the waters flow — and with lots of religious paraphernalia along the walls. Grace noticed a Swallow fly in. I then pointed out two bugs copulating on the Brigid's plaque, on the Irish word for Holy or Holy Brigid [and took a photo].

This is the coniunctio. *In alchemy, the sacred marriage is reflected in the more banal event of dog and bitch copulating. This is the theme of our next symposium — The Sacred Marriage. The two copulating bugs mirroring the "cosmic"* coniunctio *of Sun conjunct Moon in Virgo as Saint Brigid!*

Then, just outside the well, we all noticed a very bright reflected sunlight glaring intensely at us from below in the general area where we were a bit earlier, near the chapel.

An Aisling — bright vision is associated to Brigid.

I mentioned during our drive back that bugs are "cosmic instincts" according to James Hillman's chapter on insects in his book Animal Presences.

MANTIS

Friday, the 13th of December, 2019: a course day for our Jungian Psychology with Art Therapy. The topic for the day was synchronicity. We began with a few ideas to unpack the notion of synchronicity, such as: a meaningful coincidence; a psycho-physical parallelism; the cosmos winking at you; a kind of miracle; a sense of divine grace. After a couple of illustrative stories, we then began our first experiential exercise of the day. The brief was to reflect on what you consider might have been a synchronistic experience, without over-thinking it, and to then depict it as an image, allowing for creative latitude. After a few minutes to respond, the students are then requested to share their story and image with someone in the class.

During the sharing part, I decided to join in, and so settled next to the two closest to me. The first image depicted intense and expressive swirls and spirals in red and blue. She explained that instead of a literal figurative representation of her story, she had the impulse to create this abstract form. Her story was of a nightmare in which she was sinking into a bog and drowning, and then was awoken by her alarm, which saved her. It was one of those dreams when waking comes as a relief. Later in the day, she heard that her uncle, around this time, had a close shave with death as his tractor got stuck in a bog. Her image was an abstract-expressive response.

The motif was intriguing. A few months prior, Lyn and I ran a workshop for a Jung in Ireland programme in Enniskillen on the theme of death, as recounted previously. We had titled one of our workshops Spirals of Life, Brushes with Death. The spiral, if amplified, is often associated with life-threatening elemental forces such as a tornado or an ocean or river force. A brush with death can activate a more intense engagement with life, as if to say: *remember to live.*

After discussing some of these ideas, we then progressed to her partner, a young guy in his twenties. He explained that he didn't quite get the brief, and so just made an image that came to him, as if out of the blue. It started out as a flower, which then morphed into a praying mantis. He then added bat wings to the mantis. Apart from this, he had nothing to say about it, having never encountered a mantis in reality, and not having any immediate associations with it. The bat wings had loose associations to actual bats and to Batman.

I asked if he knew much about mantis, such as in the San mythology of indigenous Southern Africans. He had not heard of this. I then recounted the great importance of mantis, considered as a trickster and a messenger of the gods in that culture's mythology. Continuing, I mentioned that he should look into a particular book, where a mantis appears on its cover, *Revelations of Chance: Synchronicity as Spiritual Experience,* by Roderick Main.[74] At this mention, the female student said she, in fact, recently borrowed this book out of the library and proceeded to take it out of her bag to show us. The

---

[74] Professor Roderick Main was my PhD supervisor.

three of us sat in astonishment, not quite knowing how to process what had just taken place.

An inner preoccupation with the notion of synchronicity was met with this outer event, as if mantis, messenger of the gods, had made its presence known. But if there was a message, then what was it? Did it have personal relevance to our student, or was it akin to what Jung termed a big dream? Was this a symbol emerging from a deeper place in the unconscious, of value to the broader community?

And what of the bat wings? In myth and folklore, the cave-dwelling bat can be a messenger from the underworld, the chthonic. Something extraordinary had taken place, though we could not join the dots into any greater meaning. It would be a few months later, in March 2020, that an oracular understanding of this event became apparent.[75]

---

[75] See the follow on chapter, 2020: Temperance XIV

2020: Temperance (XIV)

Coat of Many Colours; Tsunami and Floods; Blue Dot; Mantis and Covid; Rainbow Tree; Ras Alhague; Star of Aquarius

Temperance, in the Rider-Waite deck, is the only major arcana card that features an angelic figure with its feet on the earth. Standing at the edge of a small mountain lake, the angel's right foot is in the water, and its left foot is on the earth. A cup is held in each hand, with water flowing between them. The left cup is held a bit higher to allow a gradient. The angel wears a white gown with a white square on its chest, in which is an upward-pointing orange triangle. The angel's yellow-gold hair is surrounded by a halo effect. At the forehead is a circular disc, as in the glyph for the Sun in astrology. In the distance on the right (facing the card) are mountain peaks and a Sun either rising or setting. A path leads in this direction from the water's edge. On the right, next to the angel, are a couple of yellow irises. In the Marseille deck, the colours of red and blue are prominent, with the upper jug blue and the lower jug red, and the angel's gown likewise blue and red. At her third eye is a five-petalled red flower, standing out from her blue hair.

According to Sallie Nichols, "The theme of this card connects Temperance with Aquarius, the water carrier. ... it traditionally symbolizes the dissolution of old forms and the loosening of rigid bonds, heralding a liberation from the world of phenomena."[76] Nichols continues by associating the two liquids with fire and water, spirit and flesh, masculine and feminine, as an alchemical blending that creates libido or life energy. She writes that such an angel can erupt into our everyday lives during a critical or crisis moment, as a numinous experience of the transpersonal unconscious, and that this can have a visionary quality of value beyond the individual.

---

[76] Nichols, *Jung and Tarot: An Archetypal Journey*, 249.

She further associates this card with the beginning of the Age of Aquarius, and the vessel with the wonder-working Holy Grail.

Quoting Jung, she writes that he once defined angels as "personified transmitters of unconscious contents which announce that they want to speak."[77] Concerning the flower or mandala on the angel's forehead, she points out that:

> This living mandala is placed at the spot of the third eye, traditionally the area of supreme consciousness, and in Jungian terms the spot of individuation. Statues of the Buddha always bear some sign on the forehead. It is the sign of awakened consciousness, the symbol of the twice-born.[78]

Temperance can also symbolize the psyche achieving self-regulation between the conscious and unconscious, after falling out of synch, and alchemically achieving right relationship between the opposites.

❧

Lyn draws number XII, The Hanged Man: A figure suspended by his left ankle and upside down, hanging from a tree branch. His right leg crosses his left leg. Arms seem to be tied behind his back. His pants are red in colour, shoes are yellow and shirt is blue. A halo surrounds his head. His face exhibits an expression of composure and serenity. This card also contained prophetic tidings of our world being turned upside down as the Covid pandemic struck.

JOURNAL EXCERPT 29TH OF DECEMBER, 2019:

There are so many planets in my 8th house [the house of Death], corresponding with a feeling of being flattened and trying to resurrect myself for a challenging new year.

The days are short and dark.. I've taken to sleeping late and have been trying to get to a point where I don't feel tired. I crave regeneration, and for this lingering cold/flu to depart.

---

[77] Ibid., 251.

[78] Ibid., 251.

Lyn and I went to friends' yesterday evening for a quiet New Year's celebration. We enjoyed a lovely and cosy evening at their Slievenamon cottage, with a few snacks, wine, and Guinness.

Around midnight, we did the Tarot draw. Lyn got The Hanged Man. I pulled The Fool! (the third year in a row!). I drew a second card, which was Death (my card from 2016). And so I drew another card, Temperance. This is all quite a lot to contemplate on for the year, but I'm happy enough. A general story arc seems to be appearing, toward being an earthly (human) apprentice to the Great Alchemist as Temperance — after a death of my old self, smaller self — and helped along by the Divine Jester, The Fool.

Our daughters are both at college; Katie, doing work placement in County Kerry, Kilorgan, at a modern biotech company. One of their key products is a medicine to allow easier acceptance of the body's immune system for organ transplants, including the heart. For the job interview, I suggested she mention her grandfather was on the first heart-transplant team. Our other daughter, Karla, is back at Limerick for her business degree.

I notice my astrological transits include the conjunction of Saturn with Pluto (both traditionally associated with Death and considered malefic in traditional astrology). This is taking place in my 8th house, the house of death, and is conjunct my south Lunar node (dragon's tail). These are all auguries of death.

COAT OF MANY COLOURS

Last night I dreamed of Murray Stein [notable Jungian analyst and author] and others at some kind of Jungian event. Murray asked if I had read any of his work and seemed pleased to hear I had. He asked me which had made the biggest impression on me. I had mentioned his work on The Jungian Tradition and wanting to read his latest Psyche and the Bible [dream ends].

Yesterday evening, Lyn and I ended up at Planet Spice [Indian] restaurant with Sean, with the plan of going to the cinema afterwards. After dinner, Sean wanted to get a tea at a cafe where he started having chest pain. After some drama, including an ambulance, it supposedly turned out to be indigestion. I went into the ambulance with him for moral support. This was a bit of a strange experience, in light of recently getting the Death card!

The article by Murray Stein located Jungian psychology in terms of Asian wisdom traditions, including the various branches of Buddhism. In his writings, there is also often an esoteric leaning and a great interest in the notion of the *Aurea Catena* (Golden Chain) of esoteric philosophers reaching back to ancient Greece as a living tradition. The yellow or gold upward triangle on the chest of the Temperance card could be viewed as a symbol of such a tradition. This dream also got me pondering about inviting Murray as an online guest for our students.

JOURNAL EXCERPT 12TH OF JANUARY: (A COUPLE OF DAYS AFTER A FULL MOON, LUNAR ECLIPSE IN CAPRICORN-CANCER)

I dreamed that Jung was still alive — an old man, but in good spirits and still had his wits about him. I was part of this Jungian event, though he wasn't being part of the general proceedings. He was just being cheerful and seeing some people individually.

I happened to be there and he asked to see me. We had a brief chat.

Then, strangely, a bit later (second day!) he asked to see me again. I was hyper vigilant: he was very old and so I couldn't bombard him with questions. I thought of checking in with him on a few of the more juicier parts of my Mercurius book, such as the triton on his forehead and Merlin's triple death. But then, in the moment, I told him I had written a book on the alchemical Mercurius, which he seemed happy about.

He told me his psychology could be constructed around a few principles.

I then thought about astrology and his psychology, and that maybe I should chat to him about my origin dream of the Sagittarian Dragon and piece of coal synchronicity.

He was wearing a large cloak-dress which looked a bit intriguing (strange, mostly white but with some colour parts; green, gold, and some red. It also looked a bit jester-like, yet also like a bathrobe (I thought of Joseph and his technicolour dream coat). It was not too showy, though, but fairly ordinary.

At one point, he asked me to sit with him and talk about dreams. He also told me his dream and suggested I tell him one of mine — a short one.

I also told him about the two courses we run. The dream then ends, and I'm thrilled to have this dream featuring Jung — it is very unexpected and reassuring.

Reflecting on this dream,[79] I was reminded of something I read in which he was asked what his psychology would be like if he didn't have to compromise it with structure, schools, and methods — if he could have it completely on his own terms. Apparently, he replied laughingly that, "Agh, it would look too funny, a Zen touch."

This was a reassuring dream, one of a handful I've had in my life which featured Jung. There was a reassuring fullness and a warmth to it: I could clearly feel the warmth and magic of Jung's spirit. Pondering it imbues a kind of life-energy and a sense of well-being. The Gnostic term "pleroma," which I understand as a kind of fullness in a metaphysical sense, comes to mind. A feeling of being part of a greater whole. Further, the colour white, into which all colours are embedded in equal proportion, has been likened to the purity of a post-mortal state. Perhaps Jung, appearing in a medial state between my "real" world and an otherworldly realm, displays a touch of being refracted (colours), being at the interface between time and eternity. His presence, in the dream, seemed at least in part to be merged with a greater ancestral fullness. He is the closest symbol for me, at this stage of my life, of The Great Alchemist.

The dream was energising, as this would also be the year in which our MA would be submitted and achieve validation (based, to an extent, on the success of running the pilot course). I was intent, also, on keeping the essence of Jung's work, in a classical sense, as core to our programme.

The morning after this dream, Lyn and I went for a coffee after dropping Karla off at work. Sitting by the window seat outside us was a quaint scene of an old man (Grandfather) and a toddler (grandson) both wearing a bling gold necklace. This was quite cute and added to the character of the moment. It reminded me of Jung and myself in the dream, and the gold chain as a symbol of being aligned to the *Aurea Catena*. Back home, after the coffee, I wrote to a friend at ISAP-

---

79 This dream coincided with Sun and Mercury in conjunction with the Saturn-Pluto conjunction (in my 8th house).

Zurich (International School of Analytical Psychology) about the prospect of offering an intensive on Astrology and Jungian Psychology. This As Above, So Below esoteric dimension, in light of my Jung dream, reminded me of the biblical Joseph's dream coat. That Sunday evening, we then witnessed country Western singer Dolly Parton on television in an Irish pub, singing "Coat of Many Colors."

The following day, Monday the 13th of January, I had a meeting with my MA by research student: a practice-based project exploring the topic of Artist as Alchemist.

To quote from my journal:

> He showed me his latest artworks, as a sequence of 7 colours on a brick wall, layered. Another work then showed these colours as threads against a white backdrop. He explained this image as a representation of an Ayahuasca experience, which he felt answered a big question of his about the afterlife. He described this as an experience of consciousness that is part of a whole, yet the individual aspect of it reflects your life as you lived it. I explained 7 stages of alchemy, planetary 'robes,' etc., as part of an initiatory path. This all ended up as quite an apt amplification of Jung's special robe in my recent dream.

TSUNAMI AND FLOODS

JOURNAL EXCERPT 23RD OF JANUARY: TSUNAMI

> I dreamed of being on my way to Cape Town (on foot). It then turned out that a Tsunami was on the way. I managed to find another bend around the corner where I could shelter within the nook of a tree. The Tsunami arrived, and I just felt a bombarding force of water crashing down, but I seemed to be okay.

JOURNAL EXCERPT 8TH OF FEBRUARY: FLOODS

> I dreamed that it rained much more than expected, resulting in a flood. We were driving back home from Marlfield side, and I realize it had swamped Clonmel much higher up than I had ever seen. I started wondering or expecting that it would have gotten to our house, and that it may even be underwater. Meanwhile, our New Zealand friends, for some reason, were living in our old Nire Valley house. Wondering about them, I realised they were probably okay being on higher ground. I then woke up as we were driving back home, not fully knowing what to expect.

I would later wonder if these dreams were prophetic of the looming pandemic. The metaphor of waves would often be used to describe Covid-19 as a regular image in our media. New Zealand ended up handling the pandemic well, from a pro-vax perspective. There was also something of the biblical flood about these dreams, touching on the apocalyptic. Much about our contemporary world seemed to have an eerie feeling of a prophetic end of days.

BLUE DOT[80]

On Friday, the 14th of February, Valentine's Day, we had a course day on the topic of Symbols and Archetypes for our Art, Psyche and the Creative Imagination group. Lyn did a morning experiential on Creative Imagination of the Heart. On this day, I read an excerpt in a daily Earthsky email that was celebrating a NASA probe's 30th anniversary glance back to Earth, a picture from an orbit close to Saturn. It included an excerpt from cosmologist Carl Sagan's book *Pale Blue Dot*:

> Look again at that dot. That's here. That's home. That's us. On it everyone you love, everyone you know, everyone you ever heard of, every human being who ever was, lived out their lives. The aggregate of our joy and suffering, thousands of confident religions, ideologies, and economic doctrines, every hunter and forager, every hero and coward, every creator and destroyer of civilization, every King and peasant, every young couple in love, every mother and father, hopeful child, inventor and explorer, every teacher of morals, every corrupt politician, every 'superstar,' every 'supreme leader,' every saint and sinner in the history of our species lived there — on a mote of dust suspended in a sunbeam.[81]

On Saturday, the 15th of February, we had the second contact day on the same topic, and the guest for this day was Jungian analyst Aileen Young. The two of us met up for a coffee, whilst Lyn held her experiential session with the class.

---

[80] I wrote this section on the 25th of July 2024, leaving a space for the final paragraph to be written on the 26th July 2024 which would be Jung's 149th birthday. On this morning, during my regular river walk, I came across a found object as a 'blue dot' piece of tin 3cm in diameter.

[81] Carl Sagan, *Pale Blue Dot: A Vision of the Human Future in Space* (New York: Random House, 1994), 6.

During our chat, Aileen mentioned the NASA probe (not realising it was the anniversary — so this topic must have been in the ether). But I did mention what I had read before, so it registered as a maybe synchronicity.

Some days later, I came across the news that there would be an installation called Gaia in Saint Mary's Cathedral, Bridge Street, in Limerick, and that this would be for the week around St Patrick's Day, the 15th to the 23rd of March.

The Gaia installation had done a tour — in fact, it was at The Blue Dot festival a while back, but it also had an event on the 15th of February, coinciding with the chat with Aileen.

Last year, around the same time, there was a similar installation but of the Moon in St Mary's Cathedral.

Soon, the Gaia installation is set to coincide with a day on personal and cultural mythologies with our students on Friday, the 22nd of March. We plan to tell them this story, to then be followed by an off-campus site visit for around 11 AM.

The thread of my own life myth has gone from Blue Butterfly, to Blue Beetle, to Blue Dot, and now toward the myth of the Soul of the World.

JOURNAL ENTRY, 8TH OF MARCH:

Huge panic and news about spread of the coronavirus — Covid-19 creating hysteria. Sounds like a lot of China is in lockdown. Around 300,000 people have the virus, and 4% of this resulting in deaths. In Iran, South Korea, and Italy, it is spreading quickly. Today, much of Italy is in partial lockdown.

Our annual Art and Psyche symposium on The Sacred Marriage was now organised, though it would end up being cancelled. Lyn and my time with Jung in Ireland at Killarney was scheduled for later in the month, and this would also be cancelled.

Our generation is the first to witness images of Earth from space. The Gaia installation by Luke Jerram, a marvel combining art and science, affords us an opportunity to appreciate a grander perspective. We become privy to the numinous awe of our precious planet, an Earth-Angel. Occurring on

Valentine's Day, the pale blue dot invites us to fall in love with the world again.[82]

MANTIS AND COVID-19

<u>JOURNAL ENTRY (14TH OF MARCH, 2020) PICKING UP ON MANTIS, FROM THE 13TH OF DECEMBER, 2019:</u>

Whilst working on the idea of the bat-mantis synchronicity, I came across an image on social media of a mantis that was fossilised in amber for, apparently, 30 million years. This was published close to the time, the 14th of March, of my thinking about this. Then, last Friday, [our student who did the mantis-bat image] posted on our course social media platform that he got the C19 virus. The first person we actually know who has it.

His social media post, on the 13th of March, 2020, was exactly three months after the synchronicity day. By now, the Covid-19 pandemic had arrived in Ireland.[83] The day before, on the 12th of March, Leo Varadkar, our country's Taoiseach, had announced the closure of schools, colleges, and universities (as well as a host of businesses and organisations). Saint Patrick's Day parades, scheduled for the 17th of March, were all cancelled. Following suit with many other countries, Ireland went into a swift lockdown.

The praying mantis, locked in amber for 30 million years, means this insect has been around for a very long time. In pondering its meaning for the psyche, it is noteworthy that humans have three parts to their brains: reptilian, mammalian, and the new brain (the neocortex). The oldest part, the reptilian brain, has instinctual knowledge. I had often wondered if this is depicted by psyche in dreams and visions as not only literal reptiles, but also as more mythical beings, such as serpents and dragons. In an archetypal sense, such creatures are often credited as having an uncanny mystical knowledge that can be imparted to humans.

---

[82] See 2023 The World XXI. We would eventually get to view the Gaia installation.

[83] The first cases of Covid in China coincided within the month of Scorpio (the first known case was on the 17th of November 2019) and started spreading in Wuhan during early December in Ophiuchus, just before our course synchronicity day.

Could this train of thought be extended to the insect world? Do we have something akin to an insect brain, as an even deeper level of instinct? Insects around the world, and through time, have always attracted folkloric and mythological meanings, such as embodying the soul of our ancestors, forecasting the weather, and seers observing them for prophetic and divinatory purposes. They are associated with the transpersonal, the realm of the gods.

Returning to the actual spirals and mantis-bat synchronicity, now that we have hindsight of the pandemic, we might question whether we could interpret this as a big synchronicity in a visionary or prophetic sense, as predictive of Covid-19 erupting into the world. To answer this question, it is helpful to unpack some of the symbolism.

The spiral image, made in response to the dream (and the synchronicity) of sinking into the bog-like darkness of the earth, might have personal resonances to the Demeter-Persephone myth: the psychology of being forcefully abducted into the underworld of the unconscious, as an initiatory ordeal from girlhood to adulthood. Yet, it could also be read in a broader, big dream sense as an impending wild and elemental agency of nature that would be dragging many into a drowning bog-like experience and, for some, into death.

Concerning the mantis with bat wings, we can begin with the praying mantis. The ancient Greeks called them prophets or seers, as they were believed to foretell the future and to possess supernatural powers. They were also known to show lost travellers the way back home. In Islam, for instance, they are said to point one to Mecca.

Attributes derived from observing them include courage, fearlessness, patience, and gracefulness. They are also highly carnivorous and even cannibalistic. As deadly fighters, they know the precise moment to strike with their sharp serrated front arms as weapons. The female mantis is known to sometimes devour the male during or after copulation, giving it a reputation as a *femme fatale*. They are also masters of camouflage, becoming indistinguishable from the background vegetation. They can startle. Picking up a piece of "vegetation" that suddenly comes alive or even attacks or flies can be unnerving. Not surprisingly, in China, these many attributes have inspired at least two styles of martial arts.

Their super-sensory capabilities, relative to humans, can symbolise the otherworldly abilities such as reading psychic atmospheres and being attuned to nuance and subtlety. They have also been associated with necromancy (the ability to talk with the dead) and with soothsaying. For instance, in the *Egyptian Book of the Dead,* the mantis appears as a deity to help lead the souls of the dead into the underworld.

Considering these few reflections on mantis, there is a thought-provoking story by astrologer Deike Begg. In her book, *Synchronicity,* she recounts an encounter with a mantis, in relation to Jung's friend Sir Laurens van der Post:[84]

> The most remarkable synchronicity occurred one afternoon after my husband had been reading Sir Lauren's van der Post's account of how Jung had announced his death to him by means of a seagull while he was on a liner headed for South Africa. Van der Post himself had died shortly before our holiday and in his last letter to my husband he had said, 'We shall meet before long.' While my husband was dozing he became aware of a praying mantis crawling across the fly screen of the window, its triangular face peering at him. None of us had ever seen a mantis in Majorca before. The next passage read in the book alluded to the Kalahari Bushmen, of whom van der Post had been a great and knowledgeable friend, and whose totem animal, the praying mantis, he shared. After his sleep, my husband continued to read and in the next paragraph found the only reference to a mantis in the book. Van der Post always kept his word and with supreme courtesy was clearly saying his farewell.[85]

Moving now to bats,[86] we read in *The Book of Symbols*:

> Bats carry our projections of a "reverse" order that forces our perspective into the nocturnal, the underworld, and the equivalent cavernous depths of psyche. The twilight emergence of bats

---

[84] Van der Post was instrumental in setting up the Southern African Association of Jungian Analysts, whose regular journal was titled Mantis. He has written of mantis as the Khoi's trickster god.

[85] Deike Begg, *Synchronicity: The Promise of Coincidence* (London: HarperCollins Publishers, 2001), 24.

[86] Noteworthy here is that the Covid-19 virus is derivative from bats.

in the thousands or millions to forage embodies for us the concealed, primordial forces of the netherworld breaking out in expansive liberation. Fantasy has associated bats with the New Moon, Full Moon and spirit realm, and thus with sorcery, enchantment and witchcraft ... Alchemy sometimes depicted the mercurial spirit of the unconscious with bat wings. It is a way of conveying not only psyche's darkness, mystery and ambivalence, but also its provision and unforeseen agency, the way it can lead consciousness into spheres requiring a different kind of orientation and in which can be found the fructifying unconventionality of nature ... Embroidery on a Chinese imperial robe depicts bats in swift, darting flight above ocean waves that spiral and surge in a corresponding skyward momentum of joy. A woman would have worn this "happy occasion" robe for celebrations such as birthdays or anniversaries; the bats are emblematic of longevity and blessing.[87]

These brief amplificatory excursions into the key images give a sense of a symbolic meaning, such as the unexpected appearance of a divine messenger alerting us to an impending *Umbra Mundi* (shadow of the world).[88] Murray Stein, in an interview on the pandemic, describes the *Umbra Mundi* as follows:

> Its most essential features are invisibility, universality, and numinosity. Because Coronavirus moves among us invisibly, is found on all continents, and strikes us as awesome and powerful, it represents the *Umbra Mundi*. We don't know who has it or if we have it ourselves. It is everywhere, in all parts of the world, and it instils fear in the collective psyche, which we all feel. Moreover, as Rudolf Otto says about the numinous experience, it is awesome. The perception of *Umbra Mundi* makes us shudder. It is a *mysterium tremendum et fascinans*, and it infects us with a mysterious terror and sense of vulnerability. We are not in control, and it is cold and relentless.[89]

As Stein mentioned in his interview, "usually we think of the '*anima mundi*' as a loving presence, like a mother that con-

---

[87] Ami Ronnberg and Kathleen Martin, eds., *The Book of Symbols: Reflections on Archetypal Images* (Cologne: Taschen; New York: Archive for Research in Archetypal Symbolism, 2010), 295.

[88] Murray Stein, "A World Shadow: COVID 19," interviewed by Robert S. Henderson, Chiron Publications, March 2020, https://chironpublications.com/a-world-shadow-covid-19/.

[89] Ibid.

nects people, but in this case it is the shadow that is connecting us. This is a big surprise!"[90]

What comes to mind are two of the main symptoms of Covid-19: a high temperature and a dry cough. Could this be the current state of crisis of the *Anima Mundi* inflected into symptomatic individuals? A high temperature could be a symptom of global warming, and a dry cough representing the recent forest fires and large-scale deforestation (forests as the "lungs" of the earth).

Back to the images: the unconscious has here presented us with an enigmatic symbol, prospectively hinting at the future unfolding of a major event. It might also be trickster mantis giving us a clue of the world soul in a new cycle of re-patterning. Mantis could also be signalling the direction for a home-coming: that of inwardness, of a valuing of the unconscious.[91] Through this inwardness, a newfound appreciation and re-enchantment of the world and of our place within it might be awakened.

On the 5th of April, during a video class with our Art, Psyche and the Creative Imagination class, we did a Tarot draw of 5 cards, based on the question: Could the *Anima Mundi* (soul of the world) give a message about our current world situation? Using a basic cross formation, we got: Central card: The Magician (essence), lower card The Moon (deep unconscious), 3rd card, on the left, The Wheel of Fortune (the past); 4th card, at the top, The Hanged Man (present), and the 5th card on the right as Strength (the future).

Inspired by the dream I had of Murray Stein earlier in the year, I decided to invite him as an online guest lecturer, which he graciously accepted. Bold and brazen, I further suggested he include a reading of our Tarot spread. He did a most intriguing reading of the oracle.

---

90 Ibid.

91 13th of December 2019 — the Sun is in close conjunction (within two degrees) celestial longitude of Ras Alhague, the brightest fixed star in the constellation Ophiuchus, the serpent charmer. This star, on his forehead, is symbolic of the third eye as inner intuition. A Full Moon occurred the day before.

We're still in lockdown but allowed a daily walk within 2km of home, and can go to shops for essentials. Still, the family of 4 of us is living in relative peace and quiet.

I'm going for almost daily river walks, sometimes with Lyn, which is really nice — especially with the less traffic, smoke, and noise. Girls have their routine — breakfast, gym [in the lounge], Netflix, walk, dinner, Zoom party. I've been doing loads of one-on-one zoom meetings with my students, and also class Zooms.

Covid update: European death toll passes 100,000. 41 deaths in Ireland in the past 24 hours. 630 new cases plus backlog of 148. Total in Ireland 14 758.

Worldwide — more than 2.2 million infected. Death toll > 155,000.

We told Ireland's curve has been flattened, and no peak is expected.

Trump in the USA, we see the playing out of one tragic mess.

Journal excerpt, 29ᵀᴴ of May:

We are being phased out of the lockdown, and are now allowed out for up to 5km from home. Still, 2m social distancing is enforced. Bars, cafes, restaurants, and all non-essential services are still closed..

The Global pandemic apparently now has ~ 6 million infected, and ~ 362,028 deaths. There are plenty of conspiracy theories. Chinese WMD [Weapons of Mass Destruction]? American WMD? We wonder if the pandemic is used as an excuse to create totalitarian states, loss of citizenship rights, 5G roll out, vaccines, and so forth.

Rainbow Tree

Journal excerpt, 18ᵀᴴ of October:

It's been a busy time settling back into work with the new normal. Four of my five work days are now online from home.

Meanwhile, we're in the midst of a second wave of Covid restrictions, and 3 counties in the North are at level 4 restrictions. Over 1000 new cases every day for the past few days.

On Friday, Karla heard one of her co-workers at her weekend job tested positive — yet they want workers to continue — so Karla is working this weekend. She turns 20 soon — 20 on the 20ᵗʰ (Oct) of 2020.

Katie's friends in the house across the road at UL [University of Limerick] tested positive, so the whole house has had to self-isolate for two weeks.

I've hit a point of despondency in that it has taken ages (years) to progress the MA programmes. I just want to get them through the door this year.

On my evening river walk (at 17:50) at the end part of the walk where I usually turn back, I stood on the bridge. There was a full rainbow. The top part of the rainbow was superimposed with the crown of the tree in front of me. A magic moment.

The bridge and the rainbow reflect an As Above, So Below.

This coincided with a Sun conjunct Moon in Libra [New Moon]

All of these mythopoetic elements coming together allowed for a rich inner-outer moment, especially in light of my Temperance card.

This moment had a symbolic impact, apart from the inexpressible natural beauty.[92] For Jung, the tree is an apt symbol for the process of individuation, as a unique psychological growth process. More specifically, the Christmas tree, adorned with lights, is more fitting in that this natural growth process is accompanied by the light of an engaging and reflecting consciousness.

A rainbow, though, with its iridescence, expands this symbolism. In myths, the rainbow has been likened to the bridge between heaven and earth and a manifestation of divine grace into our ordinary world. This image in the heavens had a correspondence with my standing on a bridge on earth. In addition, the celestial lights of Sun and Moon were together in the sky, sinking below the horizon in the opposite direction, in the west, in the sign of Libra, ruled by Venus. This all amplified for me a sense of a balancing of the many oppositions and tensions of life, and of an arresting aesthetic charm of merely being in this moment.

In alchemy, we find depictions and variations on the Sun and Moon tree. This is a symbol for Jung of the transcendent function, as a symbol of consciousness (Solar) in dynamic engagement with the unconscious (Lunar).

This memorable moment gave me a confidence that some of our dreams might indeed find fruition. It foregrounded,

---

[92] I took a couple of photos to capture the moment.

prospectively, a sense of hope and of the value, as the I Ching so often reminds us of, that "perseverance furthers." On the riverside, the ever-flowing water was a reminder of the energetic and relentless life process.

In relation to the card Temperance, I am reminded of the two iris flowers that accompany the angel. The angel's wings in the card display an iridescence, and iris flowers are associated with rainbows, iridescence, and qualities of good health, prosperity, and creative inspiration. In mythology, for instance, the Greek Goddess Iris is an emissary of the Gods, said to deliver divine messages to mortals. In symbolic terms, it felt as if the macrocosm of *anima mundi* mirrored its inflection in the microcosm of psyche. Inner and outer in accord.

Ras Alhague

Journal excerpt, 20th of December:

We are still immersed in busy times. Our MA in Art, Psyche and the Creative Imagination is almost ready for submission to the registrar's office. A major milestone approaches.

A week ago, whilst reading a PhD for Pacifica Graduate Institute [as the external examiner], I noticed (quoting Mircea Eliade) how the Shaman is identified as having an extra bone in their body and that this bone has a hole in it, allowing it to be a way of seeing.

This extra bone idea struck home for me. Although I had read Mircea Eliade's milestone book, *Shamanism: Archaic Techniques of Ecstasy,* some years back and was aware of the reference, it only really began to hit home this time around. I recalled that, back in 2017, during the workshop we did at our symposium using natural objects, I had picked the shocking piece of coal.[93] In response, I had decided to pick a second random object, which turned out to be a sea-polished animal's vertebra — a bone with a hole in it. At the time, despite knowledge of various amplifications, there was no strong resonance. It struck me as not having any meaning or relevance to my life. Now, though, I became aware of its symbolic value.

---

[93] See *2017: The High Priestess II*, journal excerpt 12th May.

All this revelation arose for me within a day or two of Lyn and my 23ʳᵈ Wedding Anniversary on the 15ᵗʰ of December, 2020. But on the 14ᵗʰ of December, there was a Solar Eclipse (not visible in Europe) but aligned [celestial longitude] to the "astrologer star" Ras Alhague (third eye of Ophiuchus). This, symbolically, is the bone (single hole) vision — connecting the present situation within the context of deep time — of dream time.

I see this as a mythopoetic affirmation of Lyn and my calling (alchemist and soror mystica).⁹⁴

This synchronicity — coming across the shaman bone reference whilst going through the PhD, around the time of the eclipse on the third eye, and coinciding with our 23ʳᵈ wedding anniversary — struck me as an affirmation of our work and project that foregrounds the creative imagination. The Moon eclipsing the Sun characterises aspects of our work in which the bright light — the patriarchal solar gaze — is softened by the Lunar. This is a recurrent theme in our work, a shifting from a Solar privilege to the return of a Solar-Lunar partnership. Jung's alchemical *coniunctio*.

In terms of the Temperance card, we can observe the Solar disc at the angel's third eye. In a re-envisioning of the card, I include a Lunar disc.

STAR OF AQUARIUS

JOURNAL EXCERPT, 23ᴿᴰ OF AUGUST: (GOING BACK IN TIME)

Sun enters Virgo [conjunct Star Regulus]. News on thejournal.ie this morning "Lion's Mane jellyfish spotted on Irish beaches as annual numbers rise" with a photo of one of them — looking like a red-gold star.

Ireland, like much of the world, seems to have entered a 2ⁿᵈ wave of Covid: yesterday: 2 deaths, 156 new cases. Total deaths 1,777, total cases 27,908

A couple of days ago was the first storm of the season — storm Ellen – which knocked out power to ~ 100,000 homes and businesses. In Clonmel, a roof was blown off a furniture shop. Quite a few trees and branches down. Major wildfires from lightning strikes in California.

Finished reading the book What the Curlew Said [by John Moriarty] a few days ago, and then recently also Susan Rowland's "Jungian Arts-Based Re-

---

⁹⁴ The 13ᵗʰ sign constellation of Ophiuchus is in my 7ᵗʰ house (house of partnership). This is also the position of my natal Moon.

search." *Moriarty is very refreshing after my read of Yuval Noah Harari's Homo Deus — as if humanity is at a bifurcation point. Moriarty's monk's path toward an earth-based spirituality is in stark contrast to Homo Deus's technocracy, which is very disturbing and spiritually arid.*

I had asked Liz Greene [notable astrologer, author, and Jungian analyst] a couple of questions on the international Jung studies webinar [led by her, on Jung and astrology], which she answered in a most generous way. She endorsed my basic premise of considering Liber Novus using precessional astrology and of "personifying" the constellations.

Jupiter conjunct Saturn is due in Aquarius later this year [on winter solstice, the 21st of December] with this coinciding as a new trigon in air — so it resonates with a new cycle replete with Aquarian symbolism.

This Aquarian emphasis all adds weight to my Temperance card of the year — the alchemist.

JOURNAL EXCERPT, 20TH OF DECEMBER:

Yesterday, as part of a friend's birthday celebration, we walked up Slievenamon Mountain. We ended up setting out at about 2:30PM — very strenuous. It took us about an hour to get to the top. En route, we passed a stone Ogham-like sculpture which had a symbol [as a minimalist juxtaposition of a fish and a vessel] and the words "from the heart" engraved on it. For me, it is a symbol depicting the transition from Pisces to Aquarius, synchronistic with the Saturn-Jupiter conjunction [at the entry point of Aquarius], which is exact tomorrow.95 This symbol is also engraved on a stone at the stone pile at the top.

JOURNAL EXCERPT, 24TH OF DECEMBER:

Sean asked me to go through his Philosophy Now article, which was very nicely written. He wrote about, amongst lots of other things, the phenomenon of how one's name sometimes seems to determine aspects of one's destiny. He also asked if I had seen the Saturn-Jupiter conjunction.

A bit later that day, whilst checking social media, I came across a video recording by notable astrologer Bernadette Brady (live on the 18th of December) on "The Star of Bethlehem."

The talk is all about St. Matthew's account of the Star of Bethlehem and the three wise men. She interprets this in terms of a close Saturn-Jupiter-Mars conjunction near the Sun (in the "house" of the King). Three wise men as Sat-

---

95 Note that the Aquarian Age is interpreted differently. In one context (which I contend Jung favoured) it is related to Platonic Ages and precession. In another system it can refer to Saturn-Jupiter conjunction cycles entering the Air trigon, beginning in Aquarius, as emphasized by Liz Green in her webinar. The entrance of Pluto into Aquarius in March 2023 (with subsequent regressions back into Capricorn, before finally settling into Aquarius for ~ 19 years in November 2024) could be viewed as another "birth push."

urn-Jupiter-Mars! And with Venus on the other horizon, changing direction.

Matthew, by the way, is associated with Aquarius, Mark with the Lion [Leo], Luke with the Ox [Taurus], John with the Eagle [Scorpio.]

It was too misty/rainy to actually see the conjunction on the day — typical Ireland — but we saw it a couple times in the early evening leading up to it.

I titled one of the sections in my PhD (and subsequently my Mercurius book) *The First Star of Aquarius (1940-50)*. To quote:

> The onset of the Age of Aquarius starts as the precession of the equinox begins to "touch" the stars associated with the water from the vessel. This can be interpreted, esoterically, as humanity beginning to experience the first waters of the healing and fructifying grail.[96]

We need to bear in mind here the vexing question, for Jung, as to the more precise beginning of the Age of Aquarius (his opinion changes throughout the course of his later life). The Aquarian Age for Jung, though, is clearly evident in his illuminated manuscript as *Liber Novus*. On the very first page, the frontispiece, there is a large star with one of its rays pointing to the opening sentence, "The Way of What is to Come."

Back in the early spring of 2010, deep into my PhD research, I went on a mini-retreat by myself, to house-sit for a friend at Killaloe, on the lakeside of Lough Derg, accompanied by our recent purchase of *The Red Book (Liber Novus)*. After a couple of days or so, accompanied by some unusual experiences I'd rather not recount, my perspective on *Liber Novus* fell into place. In a nutshell, it corroborated my research along the lines of Jung's great interest in the shifting of the Ages from the Age of Pisces to the Age of Aquarius. I noted, for instance, that this large Star on the frontispiece was located on the glyph for Aquarius in a wavy band along the sky, along with other astrological constellation glyphs. However, the sequence appears not according to the ordinary year (for in-

---

[96] Mathew Mather, *The Alchemical Mercurius: Esoteric Symbol of Jung's Life and Works* (London: Routledge, 2014), 179.

stance, Sagittarius-Capricorn-Aquarius-Pisces) but according to the *Great Year*, which goes in the reverse sequence (Pisces-Aquarius-Capricorn-Sagittarius). This was but one revelation, amongst a range of others, that would allow me to interpret this text along the lines of *Liber Novus* as I tried to articulate as clearly as possible in the PhD and subsequent Mercurius book.

Some weeks later, during my annual supervisory meeting at the University of Essex, I brought along a printout of this frontispiece and showed it to the three esteemed members of my supervisory team. This was a notable moment, as I got the distinct feeling of my esoteric perspective suddenly having validity, even if this was only of historical significance. From this moment onward, I felt supported and energised to follow through on what was anyway "coming through" as research with soul in mind, as our good friend Robert Romanyshyn would put it.

The current Saturn-Jupiter conjunction on the winter solstice, 2020, at a personal level, was taking place in my 9th house. This is the house of further education, of new adventures, and of expansive explorations, both inner and outer. The big birthing project was the MA, being born with many a labour pain. Our more avant-garde methodologies included Rowland's Jungian Arts-Based Research" (2019), and Romanyshyn's "Wounded Researcher: Research with Soul in Mind" (2007).

2021: The Lovers (VI)

Sea Potatoes; Umbra Mundi; Heron Encounters; Cherry Blossoms; Sacred Marriage; A Green Thread; Birth of Mercurius Child; Golden Flower; Subtle Body

The Lovers in the Rider-Waite Tarot deck: a naked man and woman are foregrounded in a scene reminiscent of Eden and innocence. Behind the woman is the Edenic apple tree, entwined by the serpent. Behind the man is a tree with flaming buds. Between them, in the distance, a mountain peak. Above them, in the sky, a supernatural angelic figure is in front of a large Sun, emanating rays. The angel wears a purple gown or tunic, with hair a combination of vegetation and fire.

Nichols' chapter on the Lover card mostly deals with the Marseilles deck. In this card, there is the hero between two women: an older woman on his right and a woman presumably his own age on his left. This latter woman is touching his heart. Above, in the sky and in front of a many-rayed Sun, is Cupid (Greek Eros) with bow and arrow poised to let fly a love dart.

Her interpretation places a lot of emphasis on the triangular dynamics of a threesome love relationship. This implies, at one level, Jung's own challenged love life between his wife Emma and his "second wife," the younger Toni Wolff. Summarising Pythagoras, she states: "There is something fundamental and very human about the triangle. It would seem that by eliminating its stresses and tensions we may be losing an initiatory rite of great importance in the development of human consciousness."[97]

This threesome-ness might also be interpreted as the differentiation of the hero's anima from a mother complex. Developmentally, this is the anima moving from the "Eve stage" of motherly love and dependence to a "Helen stage" of ro-

---

[97] Nichols, *Jung and Tarot: An Archetypal Journey*, 133.

mantic and sexual love. Nichols writes: "At the symbolic level … the Lover must free himself from the regressive pull of whatever womb seeks to contain him and step forth into manhood. As at any birthing, there will be bloodshed but there will also be new life."[98, 99]

Eros with a poised love arrow can be interpreted as a transpersonal agency largely beyond our consciousness and intentions. The ensuing encounter in the human plane, serendipitous or otherwise, that gathers a momentum charged with creative potential can feel as if were orchestrated by the gods. There can be a wild energy in this and a vivification of life. The containing alchemical *vas* and processes can be a useful symbol to allow for its transformative dynamic in the divine fire, whether it be platonic and boundaried or sexual and erotic.

In the fateful case of Lyn and me, destiny landed us soul work that I could not have imagined back in those Bohemian years of our twenties. Running our courses over the past few years is, in a significant way, our alchemical opus. It provides a cornucopia of *prima materia* in all its tensions and potencies. It is an incandescent and holy matter.

～

JOURNAL EXCERPT, 1ST OF JANUARY (FRIDAY):

Covid numbers are escalating as we are now back to a strict level 5 lockdown. Only essential businesses are open, no home visitors allowed, masks are compulsory, and we are restricted to within 5 km of our homes. Travel is prohibited.

Brexit officially kicks in today.

We went to St Patrick's Well to collect water and to do our one card Tarot pick for the year. At the small bridge next to the derelict chapel, and watching the water flowing under the bridge, we did our card picks. The time was 14:35.

My card : The Lovers. Lyn's card: Strength.

---

98 Ibid.

99 At a more differentiated level, according to Jung, the anima evolves into a spiritual/religious figure that could be personified, for instance, as Mary (Holy or the Magdalene!). A further development finds expression in figures of the mystical feminine, such as the gnostic Sophia.

Venus transit today is conjunct [celestial longitude] fixed star Ras Alhague. This concerns both mystic vision and love.

Moon transit was conjunct my natal Sun in Leo.

Over the mid-winter break, and in response to my card, The Lovers, we watched a number of romance movies. This — including good romantic comedies — is a genre I am quite fond of. A more serious film we watched was *Luxor* (2020), which is about a British woman burnt out from her work as a doctor with victims of the Syrian war. A trip to Egypt, where she encounters an old flame, provides the liminal setting for her life at a crossroads.

Another film we watched was *Live Twice, Love Once* (2019), which is about a retired professor of mathematics (whose wife had died) suffering progressively from Alzheimer's. It concerns a journey to find a childhood love, with help from his supportive family. It is a lovely, touching film, with mathematical symbols such as *pi* and infinity invoked in an ingenious way.

Around the 5th of January, I was invited by ISAP-Zurich organisers to deliver an online session for a Synchronicity: Mind and Matter programme. I ended up proposing the topic of Tarot and Synchronicity: Reading the World as Symbol, to be delivered in March.

SEA POTATOES

JOURNAL EXCERPT, 10TH OF JANUARY (SUNDAY):

Yesterday afternoon we had an online dream group with Lyn, David, Grace, and me, with a view to meeting on the first Saturday of each month. I called us the "Sea Potatoes," based on Grace's beach found object on New Years Day as a sea potato shell, which has a natural pentagram inscribed on it.

On New Year's Day, Venus was 21-degree Sagittarius [aligned, based on celestial longitude, with fixed star Ras Alhague] by the foot of Ophiuchus/ Asclepius. (Grace did a Tarot card draw and got The Devil).

The sea potato, also known as a heart urchin, lives a few centimetres deep into the sand and on the seashore. It is a heart-shaped shell that features a prominent pentacle as a five-pointed star on its upper side, reminiscent of a starfish.

This was particularly noteworthy for me, as the planet Venus inscribes a path relative to the Earth that forms a five-petalled shape (and an 8-year cycle). This constituted an As Above, So Below moment as a poetic affinity, or as a magical correspondence. Sea potato below, planet Venus above. Sea potato at Grace's foot, Venus at the foot of Ophiuchus, and an alignment of the creative imagination in the forehead (Ras Alhague). The Devil card in the Rider-Waite deck has a pentagram on the forehead of the central supernatural devil figure.

This rather arcane-sounding combination portrays something of a humbling connection to our earth. Walking along the seashore, one of my favourite things to do, allows for a revery on the mystery and infinitude of existence. In a similar yet different way, this is what our dream group is about. By sharing our dreams, synchronicities, and lives, it begins to feel as if we are in communion with something greater and more profound than ourselves. I consider it an engagement with the *Anima Mundi* and toward the rediscovery of an ancient "dragon language." In another form, I believe *Anima Mundi* can be our love-muse, inflected and embodied in a loved one.

Umbra Mundi

Grace's Devil Card reminded me of *The Plague* (1898), by the artist Arnold Bocklin. It depicts a large, sinister figure riding a monstrous chimera, with prominent bat wings, through the streets. This chimes with Murray Stein's description of the pandemic as an *Umbra Mundi* (shadow of the world). To quote from an interview from March 2020, he states:

> What are we learning from it? This remains to be seen. I have no doubt that we have been handed an opportunity for a vast transformation of consciousness on a general collective level. Many people are talking about that possibility. On a deeper level, there may be a transformation afoot in the collective unconscious. I take this appearance of Umbra Mundi as synchronistic. It was predicted by astrologers. It is timely, and we have to discover it's meaning. This will emerge over a long period of time.

Remember that we are at only the beginning of the Aquarian Age. Jung thought it would take 600 years for the new God image to come fully into view. This passage through the valley of the shadow of death is a transit, and it will take time. We aren't used to thinking in such a long term perspective. We want a fix and we want it now. Maybe the first lesson to learn is patience. A new humanity is being born. Its brain cells have not yet been fully formed and interconnected. It's just barely creeping into sight.[100]

JOURNAL EXCERPT, 10TH OF JANUARY (CONTINUED):

Last night I dreamed of walking along my usual river walk, toward Carrick on Suir from Clonmel. A bit before the bridge, I suddenly almost walked into this unnaturally large spider web directly in my path. It was quite beautiful with its circumambulatory mandala clearly visible, with droplets of dew. It was quite startling. I then woke up.

The dream reminds me of an image of a spider web in one of Jung's alchemical volumes, where he wrote about Maya and a circumambulation of the Self. I wonder if this could also have something to do with Covid?

There are 6,888 new Covid cases today in the Republic of Ireland, and 8 deaths.

A Trump drama, after his supporters stormed Capitol Hill earlier in the week.

JOURNAL EXCERPT, 23RD OF JANUARY (SATURDAY):

The 21st saw the inauguration of a new president, Joe Biden. It felt as if the whole earth breathed a sigh of relief. We are back in the Paris Agreement.

An Aquarian moment, with the Sun in the 1st degree of Aquarius, where the Saturn-Jupiter conjunction was earlier in December.

On the same day, Lucy managed to submit her PhD documentation, on the topic of "Re-imagining the Irish Vessel of Everlasting Abundance."

JOURNAL EXCERPT, 13TH OF FEBRUARY (SATURDAY):

We are still in lockdown at level 5. I've only been to work briefly once since the semester began. Everything is now almost completely online. My (Heron) nature quite likes the simpler lifestyle, though it's also quite fatiguing.

Ireland is now in its 3rd wave of the pandemic with over 200,000 Covid cases. Yesterday, Covid news in the Republic of Ireland included 23 deaths, with 921 new cases. Total death toll so far in the country is now at 3,865.

---

[100] Ibid.

Heron Encounters

Journal excerpt, 16th of February (Shrove – Pancake Tuesday; Heron – first encounter):

I agreed to meet Sean Moran for a coffee in town by the Quays at 3PM today.

We were chatting about the church and the Joker, and the Cathedral and The Fool synchronicities when Sean pointed to a Heron flying past along the river, toward the sunset direction. In looking at the part of the sky along the same line of sight as the Heron, I noticed the crescent Moon. This, once the symbolism was revealed, proved a rather intriguing synchronicity.

When a synchronicity occurs, I sometimes take a photo and also a screenshot of an astrological chart [an app on my phone] at that precise moment. It turns out this photo and screenshot — a little after the Heron event — was at precisely 3:34PM, meaning the Heron passing by very likely happened at 3:33PM.

At this time, Mercury was the next planet about to descend below the horizon.

I pointed this timing out to Sean, as we share an interest in the Trinity, albeit from vastly differing worldviews: his interest as the Christian Trinity, and mine as the legendary founder of Western alchemy, as Hermes Trismegistus (his trinitarian nature has been interpreted in various ways, such as King, Priest, and Philosopher, but also as the three arcane arts of Alchemy, Astrology, and Magic). Sean's more Solar Christian Trinity contrasts with my more Lunar (subterranean, nocturnal) interest in Hermes Trismegistus. Blurring one's critical eyes somewhat, one might consider these as two interlocking trinities or triangles to form a Seal of Solomon, a symbol of a marriage of Sun and Moon. The numeric symbolism of six here coincides with The Lovers: VI.

In amplifying the heron for Sean, I pointed out its mostly solitary life at the river's edge, fishing with its long beak. Anthropomorphised, it has a resemblance to a monk or Holy One in a coat (which perhaps has given it mythological and folkloric associations with wisdom). In psychological terms, water is a symbol of the unconscious. Catching and eating a fish can then be symbolic of integrating contents from the unconscious.

Viewed archetypally, the heron has an affinity to the Egyptian ibis and hence to the god Thoth (also associated with the baboon). Thoth is linked to the Roman Mercury as well as to the Moon — especially a sickle Moon, as it is shaped like its beak. In the mythic imagination, birds in general are linked to the relationship between the transpersonal divine realm and the human realm. The heron/ibis, though, connotes a stylus for writing due to the shape of their long beak. In the Egyptian mythic imagination, this can be the bird as dispenser of divine inspiration, a *logos*, as a gift to humanity. It is also a more Lunar consciousness, as a form of moon-intelligence embodied within the unconscious, in contrast to the more transcendent and Solar Christian *logos*.

The timing was perhaps also of relevance, being pre-Lent Shrove Tuesday; the following day would be Ash Wednesday. In Christianity, ash symbolises both death and repentance. It also symbolises the promise of resurrection, as it marks the start of the Lenten period leading up to Easter. This would also be the day Sean was to hear about some critical medical results that would affirm he had cancer.

In my journal, I noted, "A bit later, as Sean was walking with me back, he pointed out the end of a rainbow between two buildings/alley — at which point we parted ways. I told him that it is a great sign: divine grace."

JOURNAL EXCERPT, 2ND OF MARCH: HERON — SECOND ENCOUNTER (TUESDAY):

Today, I agreed to meet Sean Moran for a coffee in town. His medical condition seems to be quite serious. He is probably going for surgery this month.

Amongst other things, we chatted about his next Philosophy Now article [for his regular Street Philosopher column] about a cat-woman on a bicycle in Brussels.

He then joined me for a bit on my stroll back home along the riverbank. He suddenly noticed a Heron gracefully landing at precisely the entrance to Hotel Minella as we were in the shortest line of sight. The hotel is river-mirrored, giving the impression of the heron as a psychopomp into an Otherworldly realm.

Sean jokingly remarked to me that this probably meant something. I replied with an enthusiastic "Yes, it does." Hotel Minella, from our side, is mirror-reflected by the river. It has quite a grand set of outside stairs that lead up to the lounge, restaurant, and lobby area. The heron, on the water edge, was aligned to this entrance.

Birds, as mediators between the divine, transcendent realm and the human realm (Heaven and Earth), are considered archetypally as soul-guides (psychopomp) to the Otherworld. Similarly, a river-reflected abode can be symbolic of such an ancestral Otherworld. Death in myth, in folklore, and in dreams can also be depicted in terms of a grand celebration, akin to a wedding. All of this seemed to suggest a comforting message of an afterlife and of being welcomed and ushered in by a soul guide.

Of course, I didn't unpack the symbolism so explicitly at the time, but merely amplified some of the elements. For instance, it does not necessarily have to be associated with death. Rather, it can relate to a shamanic crossing of thresholds between this world and the Otherworld.

JOURNAL EXCERPT: 7TH OF MARCH: HERON – THIRD ENCOUNTER (SUNDAY):

Last Thursday, I was with Lyn for a river walk, telling her about the Heron synchronicity with Sean and my amateur attempt at converting it into a Haiku.

A bit later, with our coffee and snack, walking along the Quays, we witnessed a heron gliding along the river. As it got to above the stone bridge, a Post van was crossing over — perfect timing, as if to reinforce "message delivered."

CHERRY BLOSSOMS

JOURNAL EXCERPT, 2ND OF MARCH:

On Sunday morning, the 28th of February, Karla, Lyn, and I went for a coffee at Marlfield Lake before Karla started work at 11AM. It was a warm and misty morning. The lake looked so dramatic and fairy-tale-like with a Chinese kind of aesthetic of purity and a silveriness. A number of swans and ducks were by the lakeshore. The Sun was mirrored in the lake, adding to the atmosphere. We all hopped out of the car to take some pics, and to enjoy the ambiance. It felt like one of those happy moments, which perhaps also mir-

rored a stage in our lives when things felt okay, and to have some gratitude for the wonder of existence itself and of being part of it all.

The day before, I had thrown the I Ching and got Peace [hexagram 11]. Yin on top of Yang, as the interpenetration of heaven and earth. After our coffee, we then drove to drop Karla off at work. As we drove along the lake, I remarked about the good occasion, calling it a "cherry blossom moment."

A few seconds later, we passed a cherry tree in new pink spring blossoms. It was a contented, synchronistic Zen Moment.[101] This was also after a spring Full Moon (Sun in Pisces in opposition to Moon in Virgo). The illuminated imagination.

After dropping Karla at work, Lyn and I drove back to Saint Patrick's Well to fetch some water, and I also wanted to do a major arcana random Tarot spread in preparation for my online Tarot and Synchronicity session for the Pari centre. It was the perfect, peaceful day for this, though the mist was quickly clearing to allow the sunshine fully in. We did a small ritual with the Tarot on the other side of the small bridge by the Chapel ruin, and took some photos. The spirit of place seemed right, and the time was also good – it was a bit after the Full Moon, and our spread coincided with 11:11.

After the spread and on our way back — at the well where we fill our bottles with water, Lyn told me her dream about us meeting a large Koala bear. A few moments later, walking back, we passed under a tree in white blossom. Lyn made a point of giving me a hug and a kiss (Lover's card).

SACRED MARRIAGE

Our annual Art and Psyche symposium was scheduled for the 9th of April, the day of our oldest daughter's 23rd birthday. This was carried over from 2020 due to complications with the pandemic. This year was clear enough — we had no other option than to host the day online. Understandably, I was a bit nervous, but thankfully, it all worked out well. The symposium blurb we designed reads as follows:

> Every winter solstice the dawn sunlight illuminates the cairn at Newgrange. This has been interpreted as a yearly sacred marriage of a heavenly light impregnating the womb of an earthly darkness: a magical ritual to ensure fertility of the land and wellbeing for the year to come. In mythologies the world over we encounter

---

[101] In the Zen Ox-Herding picture series, the sequence ends (and begins!) with the Zen monk returning, after a number of experiences, to the marketplace. All is as it was, ordinary life, but something has changed. The cherry blossoms are now in bloom. A delicate sweetness and beauty, a *joie de vivre*, has returned to life.

similar archetypal motifs as a sacred marriage, such as of heaven and earth, King and Queen, Sun and Moon. They symbolise a dynamic balance and the creative interplay of the various dualities of life. Considering this basic mythic structure we might reflect on our current myth being out of balance, resulting in a malaise, a disenchantment and a spiritual wasteland.

Carl Jung believed a new myth was stirring in the Christian West. In this new myth he believed opposites such as spirit and matter, male and female, heaven and earth, consciousness and the unconscious would re-engage. His magnum opus, *Mysterium Coniunctionis* (the mysterious conjunction of opposites), as well as his earlier *Liber Novus* (New Book) could be considered an enactment and prophetic utterance of such a new myth. In this one-day symposium we explore various dimensions of such a theme, as a sacred marriage, and of the possibility of restoring fertility to the wasteland of our contemporary culture in crisis.

Our three keynotes: the former Abott of the Benedictine Glenstal Abbey, Mark Patrick Hederman; theologian, spiritual singer and author Nóirín Ni Riaín, and Jungian psychotherapist and author Benig Mauger. The morning was three keynote talks, and the afternoon had three parallel workshops in three different video chat spaces. I hosted Mark Patrick Hederman's workshop on the Tarot: Reading the Cards for 2021.

Back in March 2020, the final day we were on campus in Limerick prior to lockdown, I had noticed Mark Patrick's book on the Tarot in the library and decided to borrow it. This ended up as a "long loan" due to the sudden lockdown.[102] Hederman echoes Yeats in his visionary and prophetic style. To quote:

> Yeats believed that the scientific materialism of his own age was a passing heresy. He saw his role as poet/prophet for a new era. He knew that this new era would need a spirituality that was worldwide and age-old. It would have to provide a metaphysics capable of dealing with not only the deep structures of our present life, but also with what precedes birth and follows death.[103]

---

[102] It also informed a Tarot spread we did with our class online that year.

[103] Mark Patrick Hederman, *Tarot, Talisman or Taboo?: Reading the World as Symbol* (Blackrock, Co. Dublin, Ireland: Currach Press, 2003), 63.

It was, of course, helpful to have read Hederman's text on the Tarot, considering I was his *Frater Mysticus* (mystical brother) assistant for the workshop. In preparation, we agreed which five cards to use (Mark Patrick worked this out based on days and number symbolism). He posted me these five cards, printed out in a rather oversized format. The prospect of also choosing the order for the reading was somewhat unusual for me. I value a more de-centred ego-consciousness, as a "random" pick, aligned to the practice of divination. However, I felt it was important to meet him at least halfway, especially as he agreed to perform a Tarot reading in the first place.

He subsequently agreed that the actual pick from the five Marseilles cards could be randomly selected. For this part, I suggested our Italian student, Carmen Cassandra Sorrenti be asked to perform a "blind" selection. Carmen, a visionary artist amongst other things, had designed her own Tarot cards as The Pholarchos deck. She was the obvious choice and kindly agreed to the role.

I shuffled the five oversized cards, splayed them out in my hand, and held them in view for Carmen to begin the ritual. In a seemingly somnambulistic or trance state, with eyes dimmed or half-closed, she would give the instruction to stop as my finger drifted, pendulum-like, across the face of the cards. This was repeated until we had our divined selection. In the middle, The World, below The Magician, on the left The High Priestess, on the top The Hermit, on the right The Emperor. The remainder of our time was dedicated to a most insightful reading and discussion of the cards.

The workshop worked well enough, despite Mark Patrick not being the most tech-savvy. He was rather impressed at my officiating role and flattered me with titles such as Magician, in light of achieving all of this completely online as a group. In a way, the workshop was an enactment of a *coniunctio:* the "Church" engaging with a "divinatory muse" to read the future.

A Green Thread

Our Jungian Psychology with Art Therapy course involves quite a few guest lecturers, including Irish Jungian analysts. I would sometimes mention to our students how, one day, I would like to take this course myself, because much of it is opaque, as we do not attend the guest slots. My wish would be answered. One of the silver linings of the pandemic, whereby all instruction got relegated to online, is that I could sit in on the guest slots because I needed to administer the video conferencing.

For Friday and Saturday (the 16th and 17th of April), we had notable Jungian Analyst Marian Dunlea on the topic of working with dreams. Marian's book *Bodydreaming in the Treatment of Developmental Trauma* (2019) won the esteemed Jungian studies Gravitas award. Having read her book, I found it fascinating. A core symbol she refers to on a number of occasions is the Newgrange passage tomb as a womb that receives the winter solstice sunlight. Engaging with her book, it seemed to me that neurobiology had finally come of age, and its intersection with depth psychology offered a fertile vista for new pathways of research. The polarities of *psyche* and *soma*, both theoretically and experientially, could connect at a new level. For me, this reflected further *coniunctio* symbolism, as yet another coming together of opposites.

By this stage, so much of my daily life had become online, interacting with a bunch of "talking heads" on a screen. I wondered about the irony of having Marian online for two course days.

JOURNAL EXCERPT, 18TH OF APRIL (MONDAY):

I dreamed last night of being outside with a few people I'm kind of familiar with (maybe our Jung course students). Strangely, I discover I am holding my head in my arms, though I can see perfectly well. This was a bit unnerving, yet also not as shocking as one might expect (as if this is possible). I feel, though, unsettled at the precariousness of holding my head like this and start thinking I should put it back in place [dream ends].

I find this dream timely, having just spent the past two days online for our Jung with Art Therapy students, with Marian Dunlea. Everything was about coming back into the body (introverted sensation, and feeling — felt sense). She has an immense depth of knowledge and a lovely presence and style. I am a fan. I see her work as complementary to Jung's more thinking-intuitive methods of working with dreams.

On Friday, there was a piece of "green thread" accidentally on Marian's slides. I mentioned this in terms of how her work provides a "green thread" to help us stitch together consciousness and the unconscious.

Then on the Saturday, during breakout rooms, I checked my email. In the EarthSky email was a link to the "green flash phenomenon" sometimes seen as the Sun sets over the sea (and sometimes at sunrise). I linked this to the green thread and Marian's use of the Sun-ray beam to end the two days.

In the ancient Egyptian imagination, the scarab deity Khepri is associated with the rising Sun when the world wakes into life afresh. Khepri and Osiris are linked to greenness, the colour of renewal. Combined with the Sun, we get the arresting aesthetic of Green-gold, a colour combination of particular value to the nations of both Ireland and South Africa.

BIRTH OF MERCURIUS CHILD

JOURNAL EXCERPT, 13ᵀᴴ OF JUNE: (SUNDAY)

We got our MA in Art, Psyche and the Creative Imagination finally through the door [on Tuesday, 8ᵗʰ of June]

On Thursday, there was an eclipse — Sun conjunct Moon in Gemini. At this time, around midday, I was trying to send an email out to participants signed up for our upcoming Art and Psyche morning titled "On the Creative Imagination," but the new cybersecurity encryption wouldn't let me into my college account. Drama! I wanted to announce our new MA during the eclipse.

After about an hour and a half of struggling, I eventually came right with gaining access to my account — and managed to make the important announcement about the birth of our new MA, themed as the coniunctio — with the mercurial trickster (Gemini) helping it along.

A couple of days prior to this, on Tuesday, and during the external review panel [for the MA], there was an "all is lost" moment (it felt like an eclipse moment). Thankfully, it swung around and we ended up getting through with praise and commendations, and no requirements (though a number of recommendations). During this period of angst, I remembered seeing a feather at the entrance from our garden door to the small study. Seeing it, I gave homage to Mercury-Hermes. We heard at 2.06PM on the 8ᵗʰ of June that it got through, when Mercury was particularly strong, being conjunct in the Midheaven.

Then Friday event ~ 88 of us on Zoom. Robert Romanyshyn gave a brilliant talk on the Creative Imagination, which pretty much establishes a foundation stone for our MA. This was followed by two of our alumni from the pilot Certificate in Art, Psyche and the Creative Imagination.

Elizabeth Cuddy gave a talk titled "Hermes at the Crossroads." Maureen Lynch spoke on "Numinous Encounters with the Great Mother Archetype."

GOLDEN FLOWER

Lyn and I decided to allow a bit of wilderness and sea air to blow away the cobwebs of the past few months by taking a trip west for three nights at the end of July. We were on the cusp of our new MA project, the programme was already oversubscribed, and we were in a good space. This was more than a job. It was our vocation. At this stage, I had also bracketed off cognitive work, including the usual immersion in the symbolic life. Our holiday west was an opportunity to open our senses and feelings and to enjoy the stunning landscapes, some good food, and invigorating nature walks.

En route to Kinvara, on the outskirts of Galway, we drove through the rocky semi-desolate Burren in County Clare, with the plan of a lunch at a quaint cafe where a small industry has mastered the art of extracting herbal and flower essences. The various operations involving glass vases, distillations, and sublimations are reminiscent of a Renaissance alchemical laboratory.

JOURNAL EXCERPT, 2ND OF AUGUST: REFLECTIONS ON OUR TRIP (MONDAY)

On the 28th of July, we headed toward Kinvara. There was no reception in places in the Burren, meaning navigation with online maps could not serve us. In this wilderness, and suffering some disorientation, we stopped at a make-shift sign that said St Fachtna's Well.

Crossing the threshold from the road over a small rocky wall, Lyn spied a small serpent-snake of a golden colour (a legless lizard).

We were looking for Carline flowers, as Lyn challenged me to pick one whilst on walkabout near the café (being a thorny thistle, it was also difficult to pick). I came across loads of them at this site. A resilient, dry, gold-coloured flower and the golden serpent reminded me of the current Venus transit conjunct my natal Mercury, in Leo. A revelation (Mercury) of love (Venus). The "Secret of the Golden Flower."

To locate this moment in our current lives (especially Lyn), we noted that St Fachtna's feast day coincides (originally) with Lyn's birthday, the 14th of August. An As Above, So Below moment.

Lyn's middle name is Caroleen, so there is a play on the word Carlyne (consider also Carl Jung, where the word Carl means "free man"). Furthermore, Lyn's Chinese astrological animal is the Snake. So this moment in the Burren pierced through our holiday from the symbolic life. The gold colour of both this plant and creature fulfilled a quest for enchantment. Of further interest is that the slow worm was first recorded in Ireland in 1913, coinciding with the formation of the Irish Volunteers, the paramilitary organisation that was instrumental in the Easter Rising and the Irish War of Independence. This would lead on to the Irish War of Independence. This corresponds to the "free person" motif of the Carline thistle, and the green gold colour of the harp on their flag.

Encountering a snake (or serpent-like creature) on one's path can be a fearful, startling moment. It can activate our old brain, the "reptilian" brain. This is, arguably, also a repository of ancient, instinctual wisdom.[104] Mercury, as a god of divine revelation, is associated with the serpent. Consider, for instance, its appearance on his caduceus.

At the age of 53, Jung's life pivoted into his serious study of alchemy. This was precipitated by a synchronicity recounted in *Memories, Dreams, Reflections*. Specifically, inspired by his Liverpool dream, he made a mandala titled "Window on Eternity." In the dream, amidst much dreariness and bleakness, he encounters a vision of unearthly beauty in the form of a mandala-like town square reminiscent of his childhood Basel. In the centre of this was a single magnolia tree full of reddish blossoms and "as though the tree stood in the sunlight and was at the same time the source of light." He further commented that, a year later, he painted a second mandala with a golden castle in the centre that, upon further reflec-

---

[104] See 'A Saurian Tail' in the following chapter *2022: Judgement XX*.

tion, seemed to him "so Chinese."[105] A few days later, he then received a letter from his sinologist friend, Richard Wilhelm, asking if he would write a commentary on a Taoist-alchemical treatise he had enclosed, titled "The Secret of the Golden Flower." Jung described it as "the thousand-year-old Chinese text on the yellow castle, the germ of the immortal body."[106]

My own life journey had also pivoted at the age of 53, as mentioned in the first chapter of this book, *2016 Death XIII*. So now, in the middle of nowhere, in the liminal landscape of the Burren, and at a moment in our lives in which a grander life possibility presented itself, the revelatory symbol of a Golden Flower ruptured through.

JOURNAL EXCERPT, 18TH OF AUGUST:

Been watching 'Love Island' with the girls every 9PM over the summer. Have a big problem with all the Botox, plastic surgery — consumer ethos. That said, quite nice to see all the relationship dynamics playing out. Makes for a further reflection on my Lover's Tarot card for the year.

Lockdown has eased a lot. About 80% of the Irish population is now vaccinated (the highest in Europe). About 1500 new cases a day on average over the past weeks, but fewer hospitalisations, ICU, and deaths.

Major news — USA rapid pullout of Afghanistan. The Taliban is now in command. Desperate scenes at Kabul airport of thousands of people trying to flee. Fears, especially for the rights of women.

In Haiti, a major earthquake killed thousands, followed by tropical storm Grace.

JOURNAL EXCERPT, 22ND OF AUGUST: FULL MOON (SUN IN LEO, MOON IN AQUARIUS), BLUE MOON

I dreamed last night of driving in the mountains with someone! — lush, a bit misty, atmospheric, life-enhancing. Prominent features in the landscape are these various lakes, with the spectacle being exquisite beyond words. Part of this trip was educational, such as Jung's "integration of the shadow." I was at a loss for words — but at one moment I thought I would speak, but then my student indicated silence was more telling. I instinctively agreed, as we continued along this windy mountain road.

---

[105] This mandala appears in *The Red Book*, on page 163.

[106] C. G. Jung, *Memories, Dreams, Reflections*, recorded and edited by Aniela Jaffé (London: Fontana Press 1963/1995), 222-5.

Subtle Body

The start of the academic year in September would be the first year of officially running our new MA. Our pioneer group (all of whom had completed the pilot Certificate in Art, Psyche and the Creative Imagination) had a break over the past academic year (pandemic, lockdown year), which gave us the opportunity to fully develop and progress the MA. They would be one group going into their second year, and we would have a new first year group, for a three year part-time programme.

Over the past few months, based on various dreams and synchronistic phenomena, I was also developing a piece of writing and a talk, titled A Green-Gold Scarab: Symbol for the Turning of an Age?[107] The first talk I gave on this was on-line for the Irish Society of Jungian Analysts (ISJA) and the Irish Analytical Psychology Association (IAPA) on the 25th of November. I did not propose the date, so I found it quaint that it coincided, within a day, of the 99th anniversary of the discovery of Tutankhamun's tomb on the 26th of November, 1922. Scarab iconography features prominently in this find.

In Ireland, the word "cocooning" was used a lot to describe the need to self-isolate. Perhaps all the fear-mongering of Covid-19 and death, which was so prominent in the media, informed the emergence of the scarab symbol in my psyche. The ancient Egyptians had an obsession with death, but also with rebirth. The scarab, similar to a butterfly, undergoes a death-rebirth mystery in its metamorphosis from worm to pupa to winged beetle.

In a number of alchemical sequences, such as the *Rosarium Philosophorum*, the King and Queen undergo a similar metamorphic process. I suspect neurobiological research might one day discover a scientific basis that hints at such a transformation, at a particular developmental stage of our lives.

---

[107] Mather, Mathew. "A Green-Gold Scarab Symbol for the Turning of an Age?" *International Journal of Jungian Studies* 16, no. 1 (2024): 3–18.

This would also depend on a particular *psyche-soma* practice to unlock such a potential. We might think here of Sufi scholar Henri Corbin's use of the word "Angelomorphism."

JOURNAL EXCERPT, 26TH OF DECEMBER (SUNDAY):

I dreamed last night of being outdoors with a friend, where we had been sleeping overnight. It was twilight. I notice next to where I had slept some animal droppings, such as from a rabbit or hare. And then I discover something valuable. Easter egg-like things, a couple of inches or so, but perhaps of an archaeological nature as a treasure of sorts, amidst the dung, but also in the ground as if in a small subterranean chamber. Quite intriguing – on the edge of valueless — yet of great value. Gold?

Also, a secret (as if a valuable secret discovery) belonging to me. And then, in a rectangular area where I had slept, I started to unearth some Tarot cards, of older value, as if it were a mini-archaeological dig.

At this time, Venus was a bright, visible morning star, conjunct Mercury and together with Pluto. This stellium of planets was in my house of death (and rebirth), in Capricorn, in the 8th house. I had survived the pandemic so far, and it is possible some kind of neurobiological transformation was underway. The Tarot card and dung dream struck me as symbolic of discovering the possibility of a resurrected body, a "subtle body."

2022: JUDGEMENT (XX)

A Golden Sky; 'Scarabs'; The Otherworld; A Saurian Tail; Beatific Vision; Butoh Dance and the Serpent Charmer; The World Hangs on a Thin Thread

Judgement, in the Rider-Waite deck: an angelic presence above with a trumpet, awakening the dead into new life. The biblical Judgment Day. The dead, naked, arise out of coffins in gestures of worshipfulness. In the far background are snow-covered mountains. Number 20, this is the penultimate card of the Major Arcana.

Lyn draws card XV, The Devil. It features a large devil or Baphomet in the centre and above; a pentagram is inscribed above its head, with the lowest point of the star aligning with the Devil's third eye. It has large goat horns, bat wings, is animal from the waist down, and it sits on a solid rectangular pedestal. A naked couple with small protruding horns is chained around the neck and to the pedestal. The Devil's left hand has a downward-pointing burning torch which appears to have set the man's "tail" alight. The woman's "tail" is a fruiting red berry plant.

JOURNAL EXCERPT, 1ST OF JANUARY, 2022 (SATURDAY):

The four of us are in isolation for a few days as Karla tested positive on an antigen test on Wednesday. Yesterday evening we watched the 6th and 7th Harry Potter films together, after watching one each evening over the past few days. I'm busy trying to finish my Green Gold scarab article, and then start orienting for the year. Wondering about 2022 — nationalistic tensions are rising: China-West; Russia-Ukraine-EU.

On Thursday, Katja put a quote from Rumi on our social media group, Soul Food Sunday, that reads: "There is a force within you that gives you life — seek that."

Yesterday (Friday), whilst reading Benig's book [The Sea and the Soul]: "There is a life force within your soul, seek that life." Lyn and I went to St. Patrick's Well for our yearly Tarot draw. The time was 1:37PM.

Lyn drew the Death card (previously picked), so her second draw: The Devil. I drew card XX, Judgement.

A GOLDEN SKY

One of my Christmas gifts was Robert Romanyshyn's book *Ways of the Heart*. I love his style and feel honoured to have had him help us with our programmes over the years. He has agreed to be one of our keynotes for our Art and Psyche symposium on *The Otherworld* in April.

JOURNAL EXCERPT, 4TH OF JANUARY, 2022 (WEDNESDAY):

In the afternoon, Lyn and I went for an afternoon trip to Clonea Beach in Dungarvan. On the way driving, we chatted about Robert Romanyshyn's reverie in relation to active imagination, and about his ideas of the "golden sky" as in some Renaissance paintings, and about angels, in relation to a blue sky as we commonly see. The golden sky coheres with a time of religious vitality, when angels were real and the celestial dome was filled with angelic resonances and a music of the spheres. A divine realm. We also talked about Byzantine art as flat space (two-dimensional).

A bit later, our beach walk coincided with the "golden hour" before sunset. Behind us, the Sun was partly veiled in misty clouds that refracted much more than usual golden light. It filled a significant expanse of the celestial vault. I jokingly told Lyn "Who said the sky wasn't golden?" A lovely moment.

Whilst in a reverie on this moment, observing the golden sky, I allowed freedom to my imagination. A spontaneous spiritual feeling ruptured through as a sense of a loving (and moral) universe, of great tremendousness. It was sublime. A mysterium tremendum et fascinans.

This soulful moment reminded me of my Tarot card Judgement, which has angel Gabriel awakening the dead with a trumpet. An apocalyptic moment

"SCARABS"

On the 6th of January, I submitted my article "A Green Gold Scarab — Symbol for the Turning of an Age?" to the International Journal of Jungian Studies. The following day, I began drawing the scarab. As so often happens, the image sprouted wings and took on a couple of embellishments not in the original script of my intentions. This included a surrounding dung ball that became more egg-shaped. The colour of the scarab itself began developing beyond a green gold.

The final image ended up more of a deep blue and purple. I found this interesting, as my psyche had unwittingly merged my own blue beetle experience with the green gold. This image, toward the beginning of my Judgment year, functioned as a symbol should in Jungian psychology. It held the promise of a renaissance in the heart, allowing for a channeling of feeling-function toward a more nuanced appreciation of the aesthetics and phenomenology, especially of colour. The scarab, as with insects that enact a transformation from worm to winged, is a quintessential symbol of rebirth: a central theme of The Judgement card.

I was also hoping my article might be published this year, in 2022, as I had discovered that one of the greatest archaeological finds of the 20th century was that of Tutankhamun's tomb, on the 26th of November, 1922.[108] Scarab iconography and jewels featured prominently in this remarkable find. The Grand Egyptian Museum (GEM) was also scheduled to open later in 2022, perhaps to celebrate 100 years since this momentous discovery.[109] However, neither the GEM opening nor my article were destined for 2022. My article, after significant delays, only got published the following year (in May 2023).[110] Despite this, the symbol of the scarab was fairly prominent for me during 2022.

JOURNAL EXCERPT: 20TH OF FEBRUARY, 2022 (SUNDAY)

Yesterday, just after 5PM, I went to fetch Katie from work. I noticed something on the front lawn. Returning home, I picked it up. The nine of hearts. This is what "the storm brought in." Storm Eunice had only just passed on Friday, causing thousands to lose power, fallen trees, and some litter splayed around our neighbourhood.

Meanwhile, the Russians have amassed a huge armed presence on the Ukraine border. There are fears of imminent escalation and the invasion of Ukraine.

---

[108] I was invited to give an online talk on *The Green Gold Scarab* for a joint IAPA (Irish Analytical Psychology Association) and the ISJA (Irish Society of Jungian Analysts) event. I found it quaint that this was scheduled for the evening of the 25th of November 2021, almost exactly 99 years after the Tutankhamun discovery.

[109] It officially opened in November of 2025.

[110] It was eventually published in May 2023.

On Sunday, the day after finding the nine of hearts card, I received an email from Andrew Fellows inviting me to be part of a Pari centre — International School of Analytical Psychology (ISAP) collaboration at Pari centre in Italy, from the 14th to the 20th of June, for a "Psyche and Time" programme.

I agreed to do two workshops. This would be a lovely opportunity to visit the Medieval village on a hill in Tuscany.

The two workshops, each a couple of hours long, which I agreed to for the Pari event are entitled "A Green Gold Scarab: Symbol for the Turning of an Age?" and "*Anima Mundi*: Synchronicity and the Soul of the World." This was part of faculty delivering a programme on Psyche and Time lasting a few days. Pari is an enchanting small heritage town on a hill in Tuscany, Italy, with only about one hundred and fifty local inhabitants. The centre was founded by Physicist David Peat and his wife, Maureen Doolan. It has a Renaissance vision and might be considered an alchemical *vas* melting pot, bringing fields such as science, the arts, indigenous wisdom, divination, and Jungian psychology into rich and experiential dialogue.

This was my first trip to Italy, and my first trip outside of Ireland since the pandemic. I couldn't believe my good fortune. Everything about this charming village suited me perfectly, though I could have done with a swimming pool. The heat was quite extreme. A large spraying fountain, at least, would have been very welcome.

The week was a follow-up on a few days with Iain McGilchrist in residence doing lectures and workshops. I would have loved to have been part of this experience, as well. Some of the attendees from his days had decided to extend their visit by also signing up for our Psyche and Time programme. I managed to get a vague idea about the event second-hand via these conversations. A good friend in my hometown had given me McGilchrist's compelling book *The Master and His Emissary*[III] (which I read later in the summer).

[III] This text would be key to my conference presentation, Neurobiology and the Alchemical *Coniunctio*, which I would deliver in Zurich, in 2023.

The event also coincided, on the 14th of June, with a (Strawberry) super Full Moon (Sun in Gemini, Moon in Sagittarius). More precisely, the Full Moon would be at 23 degrees Sagittarius. This aligns in celestial longitude with a fixed star that was beginning to inscribe itself into my psyche, Ras Alhague, the third eye of Ophiuchus/Asclepius, the serpent charmer constellation.[112] The Full Moon here symbolized an illuminated imagination, as in the healer Ophiuchus/Asclepius, and was thus an excellent divinatory signifier for our Psyche and Time days together. These two luminaries, as Sun and Moon, would also be in exact T-Square with Neptune in the watery sign of Pisces. Neptune's astrological keywords include: dreams, imagination, mysticism, intuition, oceanic love, but also delusions, deception, poisoning, addiction, and fogginess.

Much of this celestial signature seemed to be playing out during our days together. By the time I had arrived a Covid situation had arisen, with a number of people having to isolate, including the star of our show, the physicist and I Ching expert Shantena Sabbadini. Unfortunately, I only had a brief encounter with him before he was isolated for having tested positive. In true Neptunian fashion, the structure of the programme had to undergo a fair bit of chopping and changing, including my slots.

A more enticing image associated with the Sun-Moon-Neptune configuration had resonance with an image that has a certain prominence for me. This is the image we find toward the beginning of the 16th century alchemical woodcuts from the *Rosarium Philosophorum,* as I have already mentioned. It depicts a naked King (Sol) and Queen (Luna) in the mercurial water of an alchemical vessel. Further images in the series are symbolic, in Jung's psychology, of a profound psychological process aligned with his concept of individuation. Some of these depict the royal couple becoming winged, which might be interpreted as a radical transfiguration. Interestingly, this specific image appeared during one of the presentations.

---

[112] Ophiuchus has often been considered the thirteenth zodiac sign.

On our first evening together at the start of the programme, four of us decided to go down to the renowned sulphur pools by the river, a couple of miles down the road, to bathe. This was a woman from Seattle, one from San Francisco, a man also from San Francisco, and me from Ireland. The four of us were a gendered quaternion in a mirroring of the Rosarium image, yet also the celestial moment of the Full Moon (Queen) and Sun (King). This experience — an As Above, So Below moment — reverberated through our days together. Pari, described as an alchemical melting pot, coincided in this moment with a beautiful psycho-physical inner-outer mirroring.

Back to the scarabs, which also undergo a remarkable physical transformation from worm to winged. When I had proposed my workshop title to the Pari centre and ISAP, Maureen Doolan (the late David Peat's partner) emailed to ask if I had read her piece in one of the *Pari Perspectives* publications. I had not, at which she kindly sent on her story titled "Pari, David Bohm, and a Scarab Beetle." It is a story about their decision to move from Canada to Italy, following a heart event David experienced, and also involving a book project he was working on as a biography on his friend and colleague, the late quantum physicist David Bohm. During a sabbatical in London, involving trips to Italy, they began looking for properties in Tuscany with a view to emigrating. They were becoming despondent, as nothing suitable was available. To quote:

> But we had one more agency to visit.
>
> As we started to walk across Piazza Matteotti towards that last agency on our list, we noticed a group of Germans standing in a circle looking down at the ground. Curious, we stopped to see what was going on. They were looking at a scarab beetle. Immediately David said, 'Today we'll find something!'
>
> But the agency's answer was the familiar one: *niente*, nothing. There were no properties available for rental.
>
> Despair.
>
> Then the agent said, "But we have a house that's been for sale for a long time. It's not going to sell quickly. Perhaps they would rent

it to you for a few months. But its not in Siena. It's in a little village some miles away. If you come back tomorrow, I'll make arrangements with the owner and we can drive out and see it."

The next day we discovered Pari, which is known locally as Little Siena. We were immediately mesmerized. Both of us had the feeling we had entered an extraordinary and significant place: the astonishing preservations of the medieval village, the beauty of the surrounding countryside, the community, the friendliness of the locals towards us. And something told us that when our few months in London had come to an end we would be back. We returned 18 months later and never left.[113]

By the time of David Peat's death in 2017, they had lived in Pari for 21 years. Currently, there are five generations of the family with their base in Pari. Maureen continues her story, remembering that she said to David, after a few days of living in Pari, not "This would be a good place to live," but rather, "This would be a good place to die." To continue:

On June 6, 2017 David's life came to an end and two days later he was buried in the tiny cemetery at the bottom of the hill.

Within minutes of his death, outside our front door on the stairs leading up to the family's apartment, my son-in-law found a scarab beetle. It was the first to our knowledge that had ever entered the house. He opened the window and it flew away and I imagined it gliding over the terracotta rooftops, across poppy-strewn fields and vineyards and olive groves, towards Monte Amiata the extinct volcano, this scarab beetle which is the ancient Egyptian symbol of death and rebirth.[114]

I was very taken with this story and so decided to include it in my presentation part of the Green Gold scarab workshop. I even gave the talk a subtitle as "A Story of 3 Beetles." The first story was an elaboration on Jung's iconic synchronicity example of his young woman patient recounting a dream in which she received a gift of a golden scarab. He recounted that, at this moment, a tapping at the window occurred. Opening the window and catching the insect, it turned out to be a green gold rose chaffer, the closest scarab equivalent in

[113] Maureen Doolan, "Pari, David Bohm and a Scarab Beetle," in *Pari Perspectives*, no. 5 (2020), 124.

[114] Ibid.

Switzerland. He then gave the insect to his patient, saying, "Here is your scarab." In one of the amplifications on "green gold," I quoted an excerpt from *Mysterium Coniunctionis*, as follows:

> The state of imperfect transformation, merely hoped for and waited for, does not seem to be one of torment only, but of positive, if hidden, happiness. It is the state of someone who, in his wanderings among the mazes of his psychic transformation, comes upon a secret happiness which reconciles him to his apparent loneliness. In communing with himself he finds … an inner partner; … that seems like the happiness of a secret love, or like a hidden springtime, when the green seed sprouts from the barren earth, holding out the promise of future harvests. It is the alchemical *benedicta viriditas*, the blessed greenness, signifying on the one hand the "leprosy of the metals" (verdigris), but on the other the secret immanence of the divine spirit of life in all things.[115]

The second story was a summary from Maureen's account. The third story was a personal account of a blue beetle, which had to wait for the following day.[116] I added it as a prelude to the follow-on workshop titled *Anima Mundi*, Synchronicity and the Soul of the World. The workshop went well enough, based on a collection of found objects from nature, including: a tortoiseshell butterfly, feathers, a golden flower, a bee and a honeycomb, a blue beetle, a spider, feathers, a piece of cinnabar, a sea-polished piece of coal, and a dove wishbone.

JOURNAL EXCERPT: 17TH OF JUNE, 2022 (FRIDAY)

After lunch, we had the usual siesta up to 4PM, after which we watched the film Arrival, followed by a discussion. After the film, Cynthia went to the bathroom and came back with a beetle she found there! In the main space, it made a poop on the paper towel and then flew out the window.

I told the story to Maureen Doolan over dinner. She said she recalls it happening once before, when David Peat was around, when an indigenous person gave a talk.

After this rather immersive few days on the topic of Psyche and Time, I then headed back to Rome for an evening and then a flight back to Ireland the following day. I bought a cou-

---

[115] Jung, *Mysterium Coniunctionis*, par. 623.

[116] See earlier chapter 2019 Strength VIII.

ple of books authored by David Peat at the Pari Centre, and decided to read the one titled *Synchronicity: The Marriage of Psyche and Matter* on the flight back. I found it quaint that the book cover design included an image of a green-gold scarab with some digital effects to give a sense of dynamism, as if having just come in to land.

The Otherworld

Our annual Art and Psyche symposium for April 2022, already decided the previous year, was titled The Otherworld. One of the three invited keynotes was Dr. Billy Mag Fhloinn. An interesting character, Billy has a multifaceted professional persona. Not only is he a scholar and lecturer of Irish Folklore and Mythology, but he is also the pioneer of a contemporary re-imagining of older rites and rituals that combine spectacle, costume, performance, and music into his *Pagan Rave*.[117] His unique costume making involves the construction of masks and gowns from natural materials such as animal skulls, feathers, resin, skins and fur, and branches.

He began his keynote by assembling an unusual musical contraption, all the while telling the story of how his Pagan Rave project came into being, of how he responded to a sheer energy emerging from a felt sense. He further elaborated how such experiences became modulated by his more scholarly knowledge and creative practice working with costume and natural materials, giving it creative form through a number of iterations. We were vaguely familiar with his work, as we had visited him in his studio in Ventry on the west coast of Ireland.

The choice to include Billy in our symposium on The Otherworld made a lot of sense. Our annual symposium, housed in Limerick School of Art and Design, usually takes place in a church gallery, which was converted into a functional space where many of our courses are run. This church and the college building around it used to be a Magdalene Laundry and

---

[117] For more on Billy Mag Fhloinn and Pagan Rave, see www.tradition.ie

harbours a dark history. The style of our approach, which allows for a more porous consciousness receptive to not only our own shadowy biographies but also to the ghosts of the past, is reflected in the symposium theme. The Otherworld posed an invitation and an activation of the further reaches of the psyche. During the symposium, some of the participants donned the masks and costumes that were assembled on a number of fashion mannequins in the East wing of the church gallery and followed their instincts into a ritualistic playfulness.

Our second keynote was Robert Romanyshyn, who had unfortunately had an injury to his hand and so could not be in person, only by video. In preparation, I gave him a virtual tour by walking through the church gallery with the webcam, showing him Billy's mannequin displays and the painting exhibition. I especially wanted him to see the domed church space, as there were similarities to the numinous rose gold image of a church dome interior on the cover of his book, *Ways of the Heart*.

JOURNAL EXCERPT, 11TH OF APRIL, 2022 (MONDAY)

Robert's 40-minute keynote — starting at 11:30AM and projected onto a big screen in the church gallery — was quite amusing. He looked like an image of God. It coincided with a beam of light from the Sun, coming through the upper church side window and striking him. This added some dramatic (numinous) effect.

Embarrassed by the technological glitch, as we couldn't see him too well, I remarked humorously about the opening scene in Lion King, *when Rafiki (the Baboon shaman) held Simba up to the gathered animals, being on Pride Rock — when a sunbeam appeared from behind the sky and "anointed" him as the new King.*

In a playful gesture, Rafiki-like — and being below Robert — I raised my hands as if holding him above and humorously announced the new King. In many ways, Robert's worldview has greatly inspired our MA project.

A SAURIAN TAIL

Taking it in its deepest sense, the shadow is the invisible saurian tail that man still drags behind him. Carefully amputated, it becomes the healing serpent of the mysteries. Only monkeys parade with it.[118]

The above is one of my favourite Jungian quotes. During one of our online sessions for our Jungian Psychology with Art Therapy courses, we shared this excerpt and then put the students in break-out rooms of three or four to discuss for about ten or fifteen minutes. We then regrouped. It was expected that I would be able to fully unpack the idea and clarify a more nuanced understanding of it all. I assumed I could do this without the need to prepare. In the plenary discussion, though, I suddenly got quite confused, tongue-twisted, diversionary, and defensive, trying to field the various tricky questions. It seemed I had bitten off more than I could chew.

This experience reverberated into my life as a kind of mystery bead in my "philosophical rosary" that I would periodically roll around. Also, being involved with modules such as Narrative and Media Psychology for undergraduates studying Animation and Games Design, I had this curiosity about the horns, wings, hooves, and tails of the many human-animal hybrid characters that had emerged amongst the various student creations. Part of the challenge was to articulate some Jungian-style insights, without sounding like Rip van Winkel lost in the realm of faery.

The search engine Bing assembles a definition from three different dictionaries.[119] "Saurian" is a word that means belonging or pertaining to a group of reptiles that includes the lizards and some extinct forms. Saurian can also be used as a noun to refer to a saurian animal, such as a dinosaur or a lizard. Saurian can also be used figuratively to mean lizard-like or reptilian.

I have a childhood memory of being enchanted with the fairly numerous saurian creatures, including lizards and geckos, often indoors careening along high places such as the

---

[118] C. G. Jung, "The Integration of the Personality," in *The Symbolic Life*, trans. R. F. C. Hull, ed. Herbert Read, Michael Fordham, and Gerhard Adler, *The Collected Works of C. G. Jung*, vol. 18 (London: Routledge & Kegan Paul, 1981),

[119] Its summary quotes dictionary.com, Wiktionary.org and merriam-webster.com.

ceiling edges. They are usually liked and are considered lucky in folklore. They feed on small insects such as mosquitoes. Some of these saurians have the defensive capability of shedding their tail when under stress, such as being attacked by a predator — in our home, the house cat. The dismembered tail would still be alive and wriggling about as an ingenious, life-saving illusion.

And then, growing up in South Africa, there were the larger saurians. The leguaan is the country's biggest lizard, can grow up to two metres, and tends to live near rivers. Rumour had it that a sweep of its tail could break a limb, and that they can be very grumpy. As a child, they were the closest we'd get to witnessing a real-life dinosaur, or dragon, or mythical creature. On rare occasions, they might be spotted whilst "bundu-bashing" in the southern African wild.

A more particular leguaan memory occurred in my early twenties, whilst visiting my girlfriend in East London, South Africa. Her cousin, with some friends (including her boyfriend at the time), were passing through and so decided to visit. This cousin, Lyn, would become my wife some years later. My initial impression of her was of an artsy type. She also struck me as being a bit feral, as if in kinship with the wild scurrying African creatures. On that first meeting, I noticed an unmistakable twinkling in the eye between us. Something quite memorable about this first encounter is that they were all abuzz with an excited intensity. With them, in the combi, was a leguaan they had found in the inner city – a very unlikely place for such a creature. They had decided to make a trip to release it at a friend's farm.

This saurian association with Lyn would reverberate, on rare occasions, during our life together. One of these was a year or two into our relationship, during the first time I introduced her to my mother. That first evening, after settling in, she took a bath. Whilst in the bath, she slipped and her back hit and broke the ceramic soap holder. The sharp edge cut quite deeply into her back, on her tailbone. In a great panic, we had to rush off to the hospital to get her stitched up. The scar remains, and my corny joke ever since has been that her tail got chopped off. Through our alchemical work, we have been working on "stitching" this saurian tail of the mysteries back on again.

Of interest here is that the slow-worm as reptile also has the ability to lose its tail. Yet in another reptilian tale, the conception of both our daughters were announced by the sudden and startling appearance of cute little geckos insistently dashing into our lives — on a morning in 1997, and in an evening in 2000, respectively.

Fast forward some years: married, with two lovely daughters, and having emigrated to Ireland. In early 2013, I completed my PhD on "The Alchemical Mercurius."[120] As a graduation present, Lyn commissioned a surprise gift: a ceramic caduceus. Two entwined serpents along a central staff, with their serpent heads meeting toward the top. The central staff is winged and ends in a mischievous and enigmatic face with small protruding horns. The artwork is achieved with a special green-gold colouration with glazing. The artist is our good friend Doirín Saurus[121], from the nearby Medieval village of Fethard. She has perfected, alchemy-like, a number of colours. This is one of them.

The caduceus has occupied various places in our home. One of these is in our study above a small two-seater couch. On a particular day in 2022, Lyn and I were under pressure creating the 2022-2023 MA academic schedule for each of our three years. This included deciding on themes for contact days and online sessions. Whilst trying to come up with appropriate titles for some of our third-year online sessions, an anomalous event occurred. I was sitting on the right side, and Lyn on the left of the couch. My arm was around her shoulder to ensure a better view of her laptop computer screen. Whilst pondering titles, something fell rather hard on my left elbow, and then clunked onto the metal grid heater behind the

---

[120] Amongst the fairly vast depictions of Mercurius, Jung includes the "wily serpent" from the Garden of Eden.

[121] Her surname Saurus is not her birth name, but rather one she chose upon entering a new stage of life (Saurus is Latin for lizard).

couch. It was the Hermes caduceus. In the fall, its tail had broken off. We were both most amused by this and took the hint that perhaps the alchemical-Hermes flavour of our project was becoming neglected. We put a placeholder for the online session "alchemical Mercurius" as a reminder. The anomalous event is a perennial prompt for our MA to not forget about this elusive character.

This Saurian Tail story amplifies Lyn's Devil card and has allowed for a deeper contemplation of Jung's shadow concept.

Beatific Vision

It was such memories that formed a backdrop to a more remarkable experience that occurred in December of 2022, and in relation to the theme of the Tarot card of Judgement.

Specifically, on Saturday the 17th of December, 2022, Lyn and I were participants for our second year MA students' workshops. Each group of two or three facilitators (student groups) would have an hour to do a workshop attended by the rest of the class. In one of these, we began by lying on our backs in a circular pattern and were invited to reverie around a recording of a collage of everyday sounds. These included taps being turned on and off, washing dishes, walking, doors opening and closing, sounds of traffic, and a bus coming into stop and then pulling off again. This all made for an interesting contemplation of the everyday, which we tend to bracket off when in creative flow. In the second part of this workshop, we were then invited to "walkabout" the college, to stop at any feature or occurrence that captures attention, and to consider any impressions.

I found myself wandering about in the East wing of the church, pondering its rather banal atmosphere that included a few unclothed fashion mannequins seemingly forgotten there by the fashion department, interspersed amongst a number of bare rectangular-shaped tables. The walls, often used for art displays, were bare. This all seemed rather apt for a workshop that included a consideration of the banality of the everyday. I was beginning to have a "so what" kind of feeling about the workshop, in that it seemed a bit pointless, or that perhaps it was just the lack of my own state of being at the time that simply wasn't responding.

It was around this time that I found myself unwittingly staring into a large flat black computer monitor screen mounted on a divider wall of the East wing. In this imperfect and dark mirror, I pondered my reflection. In its abjectness, it fitted the workshop theme well. It got me pondering some of the more shadowy and murkier aspects of my fragile human existence, reflecting a kind of imprisonment. My attention then moved from the foreground visage to the reflection in the screen of the mannequins and tables in the background. This came as a revelatory shock, in that they now appeared as ghost-like bodies arising from coffins (the tables). Emotionally, I felt a familiar existential nihilism stream through me. In this moment, civilized and socialized life stripped away, deconstructed, and the intimation of a horror as the actual human condition cracked through. Elaborate coping mechanisms began to evaporate.

In this unnerving state of reverie, my attention then began to wander more spaciously. I lifted my gaze above the disturbing monitor screen to the white surface of the divider wall. A few moments on, lifting my head further up, I then found myself gazing into the heart of the church's ceiling dome overhead. Light from the nearby window had streamed in and illuminated the space. Expanding my view, I then also noticed the four angelic figures, winged and with trumpets, at each of the four corners of the domed space. This liberating and heavenly image came as a most welcome relief to the more dismal emotions I had just experienced. It gave a sense of the numinous and of a grandeur beyond the experiential range of our rather limited and cramped human consciousness.

After a few moments, I then returned to my reflected image in the flat black computer monitor screen and the mirrored mannequins and tables. In synchronisation, my emotions moved from the beatific to the horrific. In a rhythmic movement, I then moved my head up and down in contemplation of what had now become a mystery. The association of Plato's cave parable came to mind, of how our senses can only perceive shadows on the cave wall and not ultimate reality in itself. Another association was of "no mud, no lotus" and the idea that our dismal earthly existence is somehow meaningfully related to the "eternal."

I then realized this whole experience fitted the symbolism of the Judgment Tarot card. The mannequins and tables correlated to the Tarot image's resurrection of the dead from coffins. We also see the angels with trumpets above, as in the card, if we take poetic licence to condense them into a singular figure. Billy's work, as a conjuration of the Otherworld presences enacted in this very space, added further emotive dimensions.

This was a notable month as, the week before this, during a guest lecturer workshop with our third year MA students, I had a remarkable experience that would foreshadow the following year's Tarot theme, The World.[122]

BUTOH DANCE AND THE SERPENT CHARMER

The guest lecturer session was on Saturday, the 10th of December, on the theme of Japanese Butoh dance. This topic was the passion and practice of our guest, Psychoanalytical psychotherapist, José Castilho. As I sometimes do, I met with our guest for a chat, coffee, and a snack that morning. We had already met José some weeks prior, over a lunch in Dublin, to discuss the possibilities of contributing to our programme.

On this occasion, I decided to join the guest session part of the day. Lyn's pre-session involved image-making around a brief of the meaning of this time of year, moving into the heart of darkness of the winter solstice. Some of the class then placed their images on the wall in the church gallery. Be-

---

[122] Strictly speaking, if following a chronology, this part of the story should have been told prior to the above. However, it offers a useful segue from Judgement to The World, as will become apparent.

ing in the heart of winter, the focus on shadow was especially pertinent. This was a core theme of José's day.

In the 11:30-1PM session, we were inducted into the history and practice of Ankoku Butoh (Dance of Darkness), accompanied by some intriguing images, archival photographs, and video clips, and with some theoretical references and discussion relating especially to Jung's concept of the shadow. José elaborated that this dance form largely emerged during the 1950-60 period of protest and intense cultural turmoil in post-War Japan. A key pioneer, Tatsumi Hijikata, wanted to "rescue the Japanese body from colonization after the war ... and his Japanese identity from Western effacement,"[123] and asserted that "the art, drama, and dance of Butoh seeks cultivation of bodily truth and inner life as an antidote to the numbness of American-style homogenization."[124] More broadly, Butoh has been described as having "evolved into as many forms as there are dancers ... Butoh is a complex form of dance that has to be honest. It is important to understand that 'your movements even when you are standing still, embody your soul at all times.'"[125]

It is said that the Butoh dancer "needs to be free of any limitations and improvisation is therefore important," and that the practitioner is more interested in "giving less attention to controlling the body than to cultivating a listening body, asking 'what is waiting to emerge.'"[126]

We were then invited to participate in a Butoh workshop in the spacious church gallery. José guided us through a number of exercises based on various briefs. Our rather abject, improvised enactments were accompanied by soundscapes and music pieces. After each piece, we were invited to share any reflections.

---

[123] Sondra Fraleigh, *Butoh: Metamorphic Dance and Global Alchemy* (Urbana: University of Illinois Press, 2010), 4.

[124] Ibid.

[125] Emily Tredoux, Turmoil: *A History of Butoh* quoted by José Castilho, in his lecture.

[126] Fraleigh, *Butoh: Metamorphic Dance and Global Alchemy*, 14.

The natural lighting through the gallery windows would come and go according to the changeable Irish weather outside. This modulated with the fixed electric lights within the space, to create a kind of moving chiaroscuro. During one of the initial exercises, I noticed my shadow appearing quite prominently on the church gallery wall, and I decided to playfully use this effect in an improvisatory way. I then noticed during these movements that one of the images (from Lyn's earlier session) intersected with my form. I discovered it was quite easy to align this image to my forehead, as if to illuminate the third eye. I found this fortunate coincidence of experience rather fascinating, all the more so because the particular image was a pastel drawing of a soft candlelight illuminating from a lotus-like flower. This was an image of an inner light that resonated with this time of year, as a soul-flame kindled within the darkness.

This incident took on more emotive and meaningful proportions for me as we were again in a time of year during which the Sun traverses through the constellation Ophiuchus (the Serpent Charmer), also known as the Greek Asclepius, the god of medicine and healing.[127] Apparently, by the 3rd century, there were more than 400 Asclepieia (healing sanctuaries). At the heart of such healing practices was a fusion of the spirit of place and a valuing of the dream, including dream interpretation. Much of our healing work by means of our courses is housed in this spirit of place, the Limerick School of Art and Design church gallery. It felt, in moments like this, that our space had found more ancient resonances. The church gallery re-visioned as an Asclepieia.

More specifically, the Sun was approaching the celestial longitude of the brightest fixed star in Ophiuchus at his forehead, Ras Alhague. As I previously mentioned, every year, around the 15th of December, the Sun is in closest proximity to this star. I was warmed by the fact that Jung's astrological

---

[127] In astrology this has been described as the controversial 13th sign of the zodiac. The Sun enters at the base of the constellation every year around the 29th of November, and exits around the 17th of December.

interest included fixed stars. As an amateur astrologer, I had only become aware of how to use this feature of astrological practice a few years before. It would come as a pleasant discovery that my wedding to Lyn was on the 15th of December, 1997. It is inscribed in the stars, marked by a time when the Sun was closest to Ras Alhague, the third eye of the serpent charmer.[128]

Aware of all of this, I was especially vigilant that our 25th wedding anniversary was approaching later that week. It was as if an otherworldly intelligence had made its presence felt in this auspicious and ingeniously mythopoetic way. It also made me reflect on the blessed work my wife Lyn and I were fortunate to undertake as a destiny, to tend the flame of the soul amidst the cold and often alienating winds of our Age. This was the thirteenth year of running our Jung with Art Therapy certificate course, and the academic year in which we would see our first cohort from the MA completing: a moment of fulfilment.

To celebrate our wedding anniversary, an idea for a gift emerged: an Irish silver Claddagh ring (25th anniversary being associated with silver), which features two hands meeting in the heart of love and friendship. At our local jewellers that week, the shop assistant showed me a range of rings. The one with the amethyst heart immediately made sense, and so, with little hesitation, I made the purchase. The symbolism seemed so perfect: heart, silver, ring, amethyst.[129] The remarkable synchronistic experiences from the workshop a few days prior formed the most satisfying basis for such a gift to my *soror mystica*. The ring, as a talisman perhaps, adds to the astro-alchemical symbolism, bringing a touch of magic.

These two workshop experiences in the church gallery felt auspicious in terms of my yearly practice of drawing a Tarot card at the start of each new year. By the end of 2022, I had done this for seven consecutive years. Each time, I entered the

---

[128] The constellation Ophiuchus falls in my seventh house (house of marriage partnerships), where my natal Moon is also positioned.

[129] The amethyst has been linked to mystic vision as the third eye of intuitive insight.

ritual with little or no expectation about what my card of the year would be. However, this year would be different. The experience that had so resembled the symbolism of the Judgment card got me pondering the symbolism of the Serpent Charmer.

Ophiuchus is portrayed as grappling with a serpent entwined around him, not in a combative way, but more as an enchanter. I began to find this intriguing. It is a very different gesture compared to the more brutal hero we see in the iconography of figures such as St. Patrick and the Snake and St. George and the Dragon: intent on subduing the Other as a threatening force of nature. Ophiuchus, as healer, is more attuned and works in harmonious relatedness to such a challenging Other. Viewed through the lens of the Tarot major arcana, Ophiuchus has similarities to the final card in the sequence, card XXI, The World. This card features a central feminine figure (sometimes interpreted as androgynous), entwined by a scarf and in a mandorla-like wreath. On the periphery are symbols of the four evangelists. It is a card symbolising the completion of a cycle.

Blurring the archetypal eye, I began to feel a strong wish that my card for the coming year, 2023, would be The World.

The World Hangs on a Thin Thread

Journal excerpt, 17ᵀᴴ of April 2022 (Sunday)

I dreamed of being in a slightly underground parking building. Suddenly, there were loud explosions and the smell of sulphur, or fire-explosive smell. Pandemonium — a realisation that nuclear war had broken out and that it was all over — just a matter of hours? End of the world!

In this journal entry, from earlier in the year, I included the astrological moment as a Full Moon (Sun in Aries, Moon in Libra; in a T-square with Pluto in Capricorn). Aries is ruled by Mars and Libra by Venus. This was a "War and Peace" configuration with the lord of the underworld (Pluto) at the pivot. I woke up spooked by this dream. It all seemed so vivid and real, and it brought home the reality that nuclear war could be triggered at any moment.

For most of my life, I have suffered epileptogenic-like symptoms whenever contemplating nuclear war. All of this had now resurfaced. Jung had famously said that "The World hangs on a thin thread, and that is the psyche of man." In the film *Matter of Heart,* there is a chilling scene during which his friend and close colleague Marie-Louise von Franz recounts his visions toward the end of his life in which the world was almost completely destroyed within fifty or so years. Now, about sixty or so years later, such words took on a frightening relevance.

Prospects of nuclear war appear fairly regularly in the news. Putin has been doing a fair bit of sabre-rattling, with a number of threats to use nuclear weapons. Looking into the topic, I realise the last serious brush with nuclear annihilation occurred during the Cuban Missile Crisis, with a particularly intense period in October of 1962. This is around the time I must have been conceived. I ponder my mother's angst transferring into the developing embryo. How secure must she have felt, as a 23-year-old, to be bringing a third child into this world!

2023: THE WORLD (XXI)

Year of the Rabbit (and the Cat); Brigid's Day;
Anima Mundi (and AI); Zurich Adventurers

The World in the Rider-Waite deck: in the centre of a living wreath mandorla is a naked woman in a dance-like pose. A purple scarf entwines her, and each hand holds a wand. Her expression is one of deep inner contemplation, and the background of the card is a light blue sky. In each of the corners are the iconic animals of the four evangelists, Matthew (Angel), Mark (Lion), Luke (Ox), and John (Eagle), as apparently clarified by St Jerome. At the top and bottom of the wreath mandorla is a red binding that forms the shape of an X.

The Marseille deck is quite similar, except that the nude woman only holds a wand in her left hand. In the Italian Sforza Tarot (the oldest known Tarot), this card has a central mandala in which we find the celestial city, New Jerusalem. This is the final card of the major arcana; the completion of the journey. In Jungian psychology, it is a symbol of the Self.

Nichols titles her chapter on this card "The World: Window onto Eternity." She notes that, although the figure is a dancing woman, various depictions, such as in the Marseilles deck, suggest an androgyny in which the masculine and feminine have been integrated into a whole. She interprets the flowing scarf as a libidinous, ever-moving spirit, and each wand as a contrasting polarity of energy. Her dance portrays a dynamic interplay of opposites in compensatory relationship to each other. The mandorla is a protecting *temenos* (sacred space) and also a window onto eternity, a portal and an eye between human and Otherworld. It can also be symbolic of the vagina or the labia. As a *Vesica Pisces,* it is the intersection of two realms or worlds: spiritual and physical, heaven and earth.

Nichols continues by noting that, in Greek Orthodox doctrine, Sophia (Divine Beauty) dances. She also notes that the dancer in the Marseilles deck has one foot on the ground. She cites von Franz: "the experience of the Self brings a feeling of standing on solid ground inside oneself, on a patch of inner eternity which even physical death cannot touch."[130] Continuing, we read: "Content within the framework of her natural boundaries, the Tarot dancer dreams of no treasure to be sought at the end of some visionary rainbow. To borrow the language of the alchemists, she is concerned with translating the base metals of her everyday existence into a golden experience of lasting value."[131]

In Christian iconography, the mandorla often contains Mary and baby Jesus, or just Mary: sometimes Christ and sometimes a saint. The vagina shape, though, is problematic to patristic sentiment, as is the nude female body. In contrast, the Tarot — as a veiled protest, and compensatory to the Church — unabashedly includes a nude woman. This chimes with alchemical depictions of the *anima mundi* as a feminine world soul sometimes portrayed in a mandorla. A final observation is that the card has a modified form of the alchemical squaring of the circle: symbolic of the harmonious union of heaven (circle) and earth (square), masculine and feminine, and of eternity and time.

❧

On the eve of the New Year, our friends David and Theresia joined us for dinner. A theme we discussed at some length was the first Brigid's day to be celebrated as a national holiday this year in Ireland, around Imbolc, the beginning of February. This would be a momentous occasion, not only in terms of a more official acknowledgement of the feminine within the Christian worldview (St. Brigid), but also of the older pagan Celtic (Brigid). Jung would no doubt have had much to say about this historical occasion. He viewed the Assumption of Mary in 1950 in the Catholic Church as a hopeful development toward a more balanced and healthy archetypal configuration. Yet he was also critical of this, in that the "instinctual

[130] Von Franz, in Nichols, *Jung and Tarot: An Archetypal Journey*, 352.

[131] Ibid., 354.

polarity of the archetype" was still split off and excluded (embodied, to an extent, in figures such as Mary Magdalene, The Black Madonna, Sheela-na-gig). The Assumption of Mary still reinforced a one-sided "spiritual polarity of the archetype."[132]

Theresia, with David as her colleague and partner, was planning a collaborative creative arts project to celebrate the event. This involved assembling a community of local (female) creatives, with each participant invited to make an embroidery design on a patch of cloth. The images would then be sewn together into a patchwork "Brigid's cloak" to be worn by a local artist woman (wearing stilts under the cloak). This Brigid figure would then lead a procession through our local town of Clonmel, accompanied by the collaborative artists and community, with some musical accompaniment such as drums and singing.

By this stage, our friends were also interested in drawing a yearly Tarot card, having done this for the past couple of years. Lyn and I preferred to do our draw the following day, on New Year's Day, and at Saint Patrick's well, as this was truer to the small ritual we had evolved. After the customary midnight champagne and burst of excitement to augur in the New Year, we then fetched the Tarot cards, assembled the Major Arcana, and invited our friends to shuffle. David went first. The card he drew was The High Priestess, to our not-so-muffled chuckles at his bemused face. It kind of made sense, as he was all in for the Brigid's day project. Next up was Theresia, who then took the cards, shuffled, and spread them on the kitchen table. Also, The High Priestess. It all seemed a bit incredulous, given our earlier discussion on Brigid.

New Year's morning, 2023. On our way to Saint Patrick's well, I wondered which cards would emerge for the year. I had no doubt of wishing for The World, as it had appeared as such a strong theme, linked to Ophiuchus/Asclepius. By this stage,

---

[132] He used the metaphor of a light spectrum to describe the two polarities of the archetype, with the instinctual polarity as the infra-red end and the spiritual polarity as the ultra-violet end.

in fact, some months prior, we had also decided on the title for our 2023 April Art and Psyche symposium: Anima Mundi: for the Love of the World.

Driving to the well, I was vigilant for any signs that might give a hint. As we traversed the traffic circle, I noticed an upside-down Father Xmas with his legs sticking out of a chimney as an art installation. This got me contemplating The Hanged Man.

JOURNAL EXCERPT, 1ST OF JANUARY (SUNDAY):

A bit of an overcast day and a bit chilly. At the well and by the bridge, Lyn went first and pulled The Sun, XVIIII. I then pulled The World, XXI. I could hardly believe this, as I had intentionally hoped to get this card — yet fully realised such intentions usually don't align with the transpersonal invisible choreographer of one's life. It came as a wonderful surprise. It feels as if in Tao, of the alignment between an inner state and transpersonal Other, of being in a state of grace.

The World makes for a hopeful set of symbols. On a personal level, it would be a satisfying year of fruition. Our youngest daughter, Karla, would complete her degree in Business. Our oldest daughter, Katie, was settling into a groove as Environmental Health and Safety officer at a company in Waterford. This would also be the year of our first MA students completing their degree. My first two PhD students, Teresa Mason and Lisa Hester, would submit completed dissertations. In many ways, the year felt like a golden age as much as one could hope for, in this challenged world. The card allowed for an appreciative attitude that, in the blink of an eye, things could easily swing for the worse. One's World could be turned upside down.

YEAR OF THE RABBIT (AND THE CAT)

The Chinese New Year begins at the New Moon either in January or February. In 2023, this fell on the 22nd of January, celebrating the year of the Water Rabbit. In this Asian zodiac, each animal recurs at twelve-year cycles (12 animals). Further, each animal cycle takes on one of five elements (water, wood, fire, earth, metal). So, for the Rabbit, we get the Water Rabbit, Wood Rabbit, and so on. The element-animal associated with your birth year thus only returns every $12 \times 5 = 60$ years. In my case, I was born on the 1st of August 1963, in the year of the Water Rabbit. Sixty years later, in 2023, the Water Rabbit returns. One's 60th year in this system, therefore, represents completion of a cycle.

This resonated because my World Tarot card for 2023 was the final in the series. Another completion of a cycle. However, I have never been that enamoured of being a timorous Rabbit, let alone a *Water* Rabbit. In the traditional Vietnamese astrological world view, it is not Rabbit but Cat, which I find more appealing. This would make me a double cat, being a Leo. The phrase "a cat always lands on its feet" has certainly been helpful in my life.

JOURNAL EXCERPT: 20TH OF JANUARY (FRIDAY, LEADING UP TO THE CHINESE NEW YEAR)

In a dream, I end up locating this large plastic container filled with gold granules. The container is about 1m x 0.5m x 0.5m in size. It seems as though most/all of this belongs to me rightfully. I put my hand in and relish the sensuous feeling of all this gold — and then take a handful, which includes a gold chain necklace that is elegant and tasteful. I notice it has these small bells on it. I put it around my neck, and then wake up.

This dream fragment was on the first morning of our two days on Dream Interpretation for our Jungian Psychology with Art Therapy group. On our commute in the car, driving to Limerick, we discussed the dream. Lyn pointed out the symbolic connection of a gold necklace to a lion's mane, so the idea of taking ownership of Leo-like qualities clicked. We were in the thirteenth year of running this particular course, so it felt appropriate to celebrate its success with a bit of Lion-like showiness. In terms of The World, it has symbolic resonances to the victory wreath mandorla, underscoring the year as one of fullness and fruition. In Jungian psychology, it might be construed as a new level of coherence between ego and self, a hint of some hard-wrought alchemical gold.

The bells, if we amplify them as a symbol, include a call to shift from the everyday to sacred consciousness as can happen when working with dreams and expressions of the psyche. It was perhaps also portraying that I was beginning to grow up.[133] Of course, much more could be said about this dream, including a consideration of the other images and themes. Here, I just touched on an aspect that seems to fit a personal symbol.[134]

BRIGID'S DAY

The Celtic wheel is made up of eight spokes. Four of these are the solstice and equinox points. Between these are the Celtic festival days with approximate dates: Imbolc (1st of February), Beltaine (1st of May), Lughnasa (1st of August), and Samhain (31st of October). Strictly speaking, the wheel should be equidistant. So, for example, Imbolc should fall between the winter solstice (close to the 21st of December) and the spring Equinox (close to the 20th of March), meaning around the 5th of February. With our Gregorian calendar and "industrial time," these festivals aren't always in sync with natural time. For this important year, though, there was a close fit: Brigid's day was celebrated as a bank holiday on Monday, the 6th of February. Leading up to Brigid's day, I had a couple of interesting dreams.

JOURNAL EXCERPTS, 30TH OF JANUARY: (MONDAY, DREAM FRAGMENTS)

Dream fragment 1: I am contemplating eternity and the afterlife, and see these threads of light, reminiscent of a rainbow shimmer.

Dream fragment 2: I see this girl joyfully sliding down a banister — and thinking (or someone says) that we should try to be joyous like this.

I considered these images in light of Brigid's Day as hopeful visionary symbols: an intimation of the eternal and of learning to find more joy in life, to come down from the heights of spirit, and to be more present and down to earth in soulfulness. I also contemplated the threads of Brigid and the stitching together of community and a greater valuation of

---

[133] Note that a Freudian perspective on this dream would no doubt unmask much sexual symbolism.

[134] The dream occurred during a fairly close conjunction between Sun, Moon and Pluto at the end of Capricorn, and moving into Aquarius. Astrological significations include Pluto and the underworld, Moon as Lunar-unconscious, and Sun as the illumination of "treasure from the underworld."

Eros and the relational. These were all part of a shifting myth from the sacrifice of Patrick to the mercy of Brigid (as Irish theological scholar Dr. Mary Condren put it, during our Divine Feminine Art and Psyche symposium, back in 2017).

In our local town of Clonmel, it was decided to have the Brigid's procession on Sunday evening, the 5th February.[135] This meant it would also coincide precisely with a Full Moon (Sun in Aquarius, Moon in Leo). On this bank holiday weekend, we also had our two contact days for our 1st year MA students on the topic of Symbols and Archetypes, which included guest lecturers.

On the 4th of February, Lyn did an Open Space format in her experiential morning slot, focusing on the theme of the heart. This was a most fitting theme considering the approaching Full Moon in Leo (the heart correlates to Leo). Whilst Lyn was doing this, I helped our guest, Brendan Harding, a sand play therapist, to set up in the church gallery with a range of his sand play objects. After this, we went for a coffee and a chat. En route, I stumbled upon a glittering object directly in my path. It was a golden easter egg about three or four centimetres in diameter — a rather early harbinger of Easter. Without understanding its meaning (we were talking about a visit to Jung's Bollingen Tower retreat around that moment), I put it in my pocket. On our way back to the college, I pulled it out again and asked if he would like to include it as one of the objects. Brendan said he'd mention it to the students, though he didn't at this time know of any significance.

It was only the next day that the penny began to drop during our local Brigid's day procession. As our gloriously bedecked and larger-than-life Brigid approached the final gathering space, I noticed that the Full Moon was very prominent and low on the horizon. The positioning was perfect: it aligned with her third eye. This convergence of phenomena intensified the occasion. My imagination and emotions be-

---

[135] This was due, in part, to Lyn's input being a close friend of the primary artist of the event, as Theresia Guschlbauer.

167

came illuminated during this hopeful moment of Ireland's "herstory."

The golden egg, as a found object, struck me as one of those As Above, So Below moments. The mythology and folklore of the Full Moon are replete with meanings of a pregnant fullness. More specifically, in the sign of Leo — which has gold and the heart as its symbols — it might be construed as a visionary symbol of a new beginning. It could also symbolise a renaissance as an incarnation of the self within the psyche at a new level along the circumambulatory path of individuation. It augured a greater opening of the heart, consonant with a broader cultural shift.

Anima Mundi (and AI)

We usually begin considering the theme for our annual Art and Psyche symposium in April, soon after the most current symposium has completed. Sometime in April or early May of 2022, we settled on the title Anima Mundi (Soul of the World), and later added a subtitle For the Love of the World. Our three keynotes were also already agreed in 2022: Andrew Fellows, Yuriko Sato, and Grace Wells. Andrew and Yuriko came in from Switzerland and are integrally involved with the running of ISAP-Zurich. Andrew, a Jungian analyst with a PhD in Physics, is also the author of the award-winning *Gaia, Psyche and Deep Ecology* (2019). Yuriko, originally from Japan, is both a psychiatrist and a Jungian analyst. Grace is an eco-poet with a beautiful sensitivity to our valuing of psyche.

In designing the flyer, Lyn and I had some difficulty selecting appropriate imagery or artwork. On Valentine's Day, the 14th of February, I had a small experience that helped this along. That morning, I managed to get Lyn some flowers and chocolates (and a bottle). Later in the day, I met with my friend Dónal[136] for our more-or-less weekly walk. We usually do a circuit with a large oak tree near the river as our halfway

---

[136] One of Dónal's award winning documentary films, *Dreamtime Revisited*, is on the life and work of eco-poet and philosopher John Moriarty.

mark. One of its main branches is broken off, and during mid-winter, I would sometimes think it had died. But, soon enough, we are welcomed by its return to life. The tree has also become somewhat of a focal point for our chats and, in a way, has become a silent third companion.

On this particular day, upon our return leg, my attention was alerted to a glint on the ground in front of me. It turned out to be a small blue marble, which I put in my pocket, vaguely sensing a symbolic relevance. Our discussion at this time was about Eco-Dharma and ways of orienting one's life. Only later, chatting to Lyn, did I realise the significance of finding an image for our symposium flyer. The Earth from space was described, iconically, as not only a "pale blue dot" but also as a jewel-like "blue marble." This connected to Valentine's Day and our subtitle, For the Love of the World.[137]

At our art college in Limerick, there are two courtyards. In the first of these is a prominent and majestic-looking tree, a few metres in height. On the wall next to it is a large image of the Earth accompanied by the graffiti "There is No Earth 2." Seeing this image regularly has allowed it to become engraved in the art college psyche. Yet, as if in response, I became more aware of a technological development, as the phenomenon of a virtual Earth 2. On the website, we read:

> Worlds within a World within the World
>
> Our vision with Earth 2 is to create a digital representation of our world and migrate 2D web experiences into 3D spaces. A Metaverse that creates an online experiential space where people can build, trade, live, interact, and create their own story.[138]

It seemed to me that humanity was beginning to bifurcate into earth lovers and those happy enough to drop the sorrowful remnants of embodied existence and increasingly enter the new world or metaverse. Possibly more worrying, though,

---

[137] We ended up choosing the artwork from Luke Jerram's *Gaia* installation, which we had managed to visit in Cobh Cathedral on a rainy day the previous summer in June 2022.

[138] Version 2 Pty Ltd., *Earth 2®*, launched November 2020, accessed October 2, 2025, https://earth2.io/.

for now, was the prominent emergence of artificial intelligence.

JOURNAL EXCERPT, 18TH OF MARCH (SATURDAY, SHEELA'S DAY, AFTER ST PATRICK'S DAY)

Earlier in the week, I attended an online webinar on ChatGPT, and then yesterday I signed up to ChatGPT for the first time — quite a spooky feeling — as if a penny dropping about a whole new era opening up. Some strange emotions are beginning to surface about it, such as feeling eclipsed by AI. Something I certainly didn't expect during my lifetime.

I asked it to give a short description of synchronicity, which it did fine enough. Then I asked it to consider the relation between synchronicity and the unus mundus — also not too bad, at a cursory evaluation.

After this, I typed in, requesting an example of synchronicity that included birds. Whilst it was typing/thinking, Robbie (the Robin), who I feed oats to, arrives at the step outside the sliding door.

After further looking into AI, I became even more spooked and wondered if a dangerous genie had been loosed upon the world with emergent characteristics and capabilities. Suddenly, all those science fiction notions of humans and robots take on a newfound and disturbing relevance. It is becoming a hot topic. In a CNN interview dated the 17th of April, the headline reads: "Elon Musk warns AI could cause 'civilization destruction' even as he invests in it."[139]

On Tuesday, the 18th of April, Andrew and Yuriko arrive in Clonmel to stay with us for a couple of nights, before heading west for a short wilderness trip, and prior to our symposium on Saturday, the 22nd of April. Wednesday, the 19th of April, we decided to visit our nearby Medieval village of Fethard, where my PhD student on Sheela-na-gigs, Teresa Mason, also agreed to meet us. At our favourite coffee shop, Teresa kindly introduced our guests to the hidden enigma of Sheelas, followed by a lovely walkabout, including some stop points to venerate the stone-carved Sheelas of Fethard.

Thursday and Friday, the 20th and 21st of April, were two full pre-symposium days in the Limerick Art School church

---

[139] "Elon Musk Warns AI Could Cause 'Civilization Destruction' Even as He Invests in It," *CNN Business*, April 18, 2023, accessed October 2, 2025.

gallery for all of our MA students, broadly titled Personal and Cultural Problematics. A strong emergent problematic that is refracted in much of the MA work revolves around a declining patriarchy and resurgence of the feminine, along the lines of a "new myth for our times." The 20th of April also coincided with a total Solar eclipse (at 29 degrees Aries), taking place early that morning, though this was not visible from Ireland. This eclipse of the feminine Lunar overshadowing the (old King) masculine Solar captured, in broad brushstrokes, much of the work that was showcased. The location, a deconsecrated church, was an apt vessel for the transformative work.

On that Friday, we enjoyed a beautiful presentation by Lisa Hester on Re-envisioning Visionary Art. We then concluded our two-day intensive with a most compelling presentation by Teresa Mason on Sheela-na-gigs, coinciding with her birthday. Her presentation ended with a visual sequence of Sheela images to the soundtrack by folk singer Joni Mitchell titled "Magdalene Laundries." The following day was our Anima Mundi symposium, which was oversubscribed with over a hundred people in attendance.

ZURICH ADVENTURERS

I had made a rather flippant promise to our third-year MA students over the past couple of years: a trip to Zurich to include visits to Jung's Bollingen Tower and his house at Kusnacht. Most of us by this stage had travelled a long road together, and it seemed as if, at one level, we had become like a family. They held me to this promise, applying some pressure to deliver.

Thankfully, especially with the help of Lyn, this all worked out. A three-day itinerary was planned for the end of June. Less fortunately, though, Lyn, due to passport issues, could not join us.

Our itinerary included a morning at the Kunsthaus in Zurich Central, followed by a tour of ISAP in the afternoon (27th of June). The following day included a visit to the Jung museum at Gommiswald, followed by an afternoon at Bollingen Tower. The final official day of our trip included a visit to Jung's grave, followed by a tour of his Kusnacht house museum. After lunch on the lakeside, we would then visit some Zurich art galleries in the afternoon. The following three days were the 75th anniversary conference of the C. G. Jung Institute at Kusnacht, with the theme I Feel ... Therefore, I Am.

My presentation, Neurobiology and the Alchemical Coniunctio, was scheduled for Saturday afternoon, the 1st of July. The notion of the alchemical *coniunctio* was a longstanding interest of mine, having presented and published on this theme on a number of occasions. This particular talk was meant to open a dialogue between Jung's more esoteric notion as a changing myth from the Age of Pisces (*separatio*) to the Age of Aquarius (*coniunctio*), in relation especially to Iain McGilchrist's work on right and left-brain neurobiology. Earlier in the month, I had begun to read Lindsay Clarke's *The Chymical Wedding*. I brought this text along on the trip. Astrologically, the trip coincided with a Mars-Venus conjunction in Leo (approaching Star Regulus, heart of the Lion), and a tight Mercury-Sun conjunction in Cancer.

Just as Christmas is close to the winter solstice (the birth of light in the heart of darkness), so St. John's Day, on the 24th of June, is close to the summer solstice. Our trip would be shortly after St. John (the Baptist) Day. This is also the time of year that coincides with roses beginning to bloom, spawning a mythos around St. John and the rose. I was therefore alerted to one of our students' rather stunning photographs of a mountain lake in the Swiss Alps (he had started his trip a bit earlier), posted on our social media group on the morning of the 24th. In the foreground were some yellow flowers that formed an aesthetically pleasing contrast to the snow-covered mountains and the tranquil, blue lake. I responded with a golden flower emoji.

This precipitated a conversation I had with Lyn that day, coalescing around the various meanings and occurrences of the golden flower theme in my life.[140] She was especially amused by all of this, as she pointed out that not only was it St. John's Day, but that the first bloom of our white rose (with yellow-gold centre) in our garden had appeared on this day. In fact, she noted that this small rose bush was gifted to us over a couple of years prior by the class that was now about to embark on our Zurich trip.[141] Lyn shared a photograph of the rose on our Zurich Adventurer's social media chat group, which served as a beautiful symbol to bless our adventure, and our "baptism" in the waters of Lake Zurich.

Our itinerary only allowed for a couple of hours at the rather expansive Kunsthaus on the 27th of June. Among the many greats were a couple of my favourites: Paul Klee and Marc Chagall. Klee's *Super-Chess*, 1937, stood out, especially in relation to our times with the current geopolitical earthquake. This work not only breaks sharp rectilinear symmetries but also adds complexity through the addition of the colours of grey, red, and blue beyond the black and white binary. In the painting, a large (taking up three blocks) red Queen (or King?) is positioned slightly off-centre to the lower right. The slightly round-edged chessboard is on the royal colour as a burgundy background. The breaking of symmetries and addition of colours allow us to view the work as a metaphoric mirror of pre-war 1937. This is a complex way beyond the clear rules and operational parameters of a simple chess game. In the midst of all of this is a large presence in revolutionary red. For me, this image-emotion echoed through the decades, hitting home a chilling sense of history recurring in our current world situation.

Of the various intriguing Chagall paintings, one in particular, and perhaps predictably, coincided with the *coniunctio* theme. This was his 1968 *Above Paris*. In his characteristically

---

[140] For various reasons I had come to associate my trips to Zurich with the notion of *The Secret of the Golden Flower*. One memory was of seeing all the exquisite city lights of Zurich during a night flight, leaving Zurich.

[141] As if to reinforce this as a synchronicity, I stumbled upon a found object as a small foam golden flower on my path earlier in the day (placed in the back flap of my creative journal).

soulful and otherworldly style, this image portrays a celestial *coniunctio:* a clothed man and naked woman floating in a yellow-golden sky above Paris. They are ensconced in a warm, red and golden mandorla-like cocoon. At their base is a dramatic bouquet of flowers, including what appears to be red and white roses. On the right, in a turquoise-grey hue, is perhaps a lesser *coiniunctio* of a couple of more upright, clothed lovers.

After a couple of hours at the art gallery, we then trekked through the old town, traversing many small cafes and restaurants en route to the park next to ISAP, where we then assembled for a picnic lunch. After lunch, Andrew and Yuriko graced us with a tour of the International School of Analytical Psychology (ISAP).[142]

The next morning, Wednesday the 28th of June, I shared a photo I had taken at the Kunsthaus of a baby Hermes with a winged helmet atop a tortoise, sculpted in what looked like white marble. This seemed a fitting opening for our upcoming day. The itinerary included a trip to the Jung museum in Gommiswald, followed by a lunch on the lake edge in Schmerikon, and then a visit to Bollingen Tower. Apart from some time delays cascading through the day, everything worked more or less according to plan.

Hans Hoerni, Jung's great-grandson, gave us a warm welcome as we finally arrived outside the Bollingen Tower. It was another hot summer day, and a bit of a trek to arrive. Being divided into two groups allowed the second group (not in the tower) to relax in the shade, and some of us also took a dip in the lake. This was of particular symbolic significance for me, as my personal image used on social media features the alchemist and *soror mystica* (from the 16th-century Griemiller's version of the *Rosarium Philosophorum*), superimposed on a lake. It resonated with the current Mars-Venus conjunction in

---

[142] During our tour of the library I noticed an astrological chart on the wall behind the librarian's seat. Andrew explained it was the ISAP astrological chart, drawn up by Liz Green. I couldn't help but notice its Mercury at 26 degrees Leo (known as the Astrologer's degree). My ruling planet, Mercury, is also at 26 degrees Leo. My first guest lecture session for ISAP was on my PhD research on *The Alchemical Mercurius* (and the title of my book).

Leo, and the presentation I would give later that week on the *alchemical conunctio.*

The Sun, after its mid-summer solstice point, enters the water sign of Cancer. This could be interpreted as a refreshing baptism amidst the heat. The fairly close Mercury-Sun conjunction in Cancer during our trip (exact on Saturday, 1st of July) seemed apt, considering all the trickster elements so evident at the Tower, such as the stone engraving of Mercurius on the wall, and the central symbol as the astrological glyph of Mercury on the iconic Bollingen stone. In terms of this, it was rather quaint to notice a photo appear on our social media chat group of one of our class who had done his dissertation titled The Fool's Journey. The picture depicted him in Hermes-trickster style, sitting on top of the Bollingen stone,[143] as a kind of a throne (Mercury conjunct Sun) at the lake edge (Cancer).

This was my second trip to Bollingen Tower (the first over a decade ago, during my PhD studies). A few extra details caught my attention that had previously eluded me. One of these was the emphasis Jung seemed to give to family bloodlines as depicted in the painted roof in the sheltered area within the outside terrace. Included as one of these are zigzag like formations that, according to Hans, relate to Emma Rauschenbach, her surname being associated with "river." I had been very interested in this motif in a number of his artworks, which I have interpreted as relating to his fascination with the Aquarian Age. Similarly, I had interpreted a number of his stone engravings from this perspective, drawing from his published works, letters, and seminars. This visit further corroborated the perspective I had developed. Lake Zurich itself might be considered as having an affinity with the Aquarian vessel, a symbol of the unconscious psyche.

Having the extra time in the Tower environs (being split into two groups) allowed for a discovery that the front entrance offered an interesting photo opportunity. I was vigilant of a dappled light coming through the trees, and so

---

143 Note: Hans Hoerni did give him permission to do this.

thought to include some of these Sun rays in the photography. It was only a bit later, once I had a chance to go through them, that I noticed some strange lens-flare effects. One of them in particular stood out as an almost perfect horizontal mandorla clearly visible in front of the Tower entrance. Zooming in, one can clearly discern a rainbow-like iridescence. I was taken aback; in my decades of taking photographs, this was a first anomalous mandorla-shaped lens flare phenomenon. The effect was repeated, in a slightly more distorted form, in more of my photographs. In a couple of these, one of our group members appeared halfway inside the shape. In another, a cross clearly appears in front of the Bollingen Tower door. It then transpired that some of the photographs from others in our group also captured similar lens-flare anomalies at this location, though none quite as dramatic as the near-perfect horizontal mandorla.

This phenomenon intrigued me, even if there was a scientific explanation. The diaphanous, rainbow-iridescence of the mandorla in front of the stone Tower suggested a convergence of spirit and matter. The appearance of this shape, at this specific time and place, and considering its prominence as a symbol during the year, struck me as remarkable. The World Tarot card, Lyn's mandorla-shaped rewilding project, my PhD students Sheela-na-gig dissertation (rock carvings of women displaying an open vulva), and more recently the loving couple image (*coniunctio*) in Chagall's artwork in the Kunsthaus all added vital layers of meaning to this ancient symbol.

Further meanings and amplifications of the *vesica piscis* and mandorla include their use in Christian religious iconography (as already mentioned). It depicts the interface between our material, empirical reality and a spiritual reality: a portal between matter and spirit, and as a mediator of opposites. As a vagina-yoni shape, it symbolises the entrance through which we enter the world and also exit the world into the womb of the earth. In early Christianity, it has been associated with the Glory of God and a coming together of the terrestrial and the celestial, humanity and divinity, which are inseparably bound together after Christ's Resurrection. It also represents "the sacred event of God's *theophany* — direct manifestation of the Divine Dynamics of God."[144] In the Jewish religion, it has been associated with the Shekinah, which has "been viewed as a spatial-temporal event, when God 'sanctifies a place, an object, an individual or a whole people — a revelation of the holy in the midst of profane.'"[145] In the earlier Pythagorean worldview, the *Vesica Piscis* symbolism included the notion of "the entire Cosmos as a unity between material and sacred space" and that "its egg-like shape had been used for depicting the Cosmos and the birth of life."[146] More specifically, a differentiation has been made between the vertical and horizontal forms, with the latter also being connected with the rich symbolism of the fish as we find in Christianity. These include associations to baptism, resurrection, immortality, and the eucharist.[147]

The trip to Bollingen Tower had touched us in a profound way. Anxious about our bus driver beginning to give up about time delays over a phone call, I hurried everyone up. We ambled back at a fair pace and settled into the drive back to Zurich after a most satisfying day.[148] That evening we found a lovely Italian place for dinner in the city centre. After dinner, we then walked to the left edge of the lake and settled in for a couple of drinks on the terrace. Over a conversation, I remarked on having regretted not taking a pebble from Bollingen Tower area. At this, Margaret pulled out three stones and suggested I choose one. I chose a white-marble stone, as it reminded me of the Hermes on the tortoise sculpture, and

---

[144] Todorova, Rotislava. "The Migrating Symbol: Vesica Piscis from the Pythagoreans to Christianity." *Vesalius* 20, no. 1 (2014): 24-27.

[145] Ibid.

[146] Ibid.

[147] See, for example, Jung's CW9ii *Aion*.

[148] On the bus, as we entered Zurich, Patrick (our number plate expert) noticed a 444 on a taxi (also reflected on its roof). The car in front of it had 444 sequence on its numberplate. I managed to get a perfect alignment photograph of the numbers together, to make a sequence of 3 x 444. Perhaps a trickster's wink to end our day (in light of Bollingen Tower symbolism being imbued with Jung's renowned 3-4 number fascination).

the image I had posted in our social media group that morning. When I mentioned this, she insisted I also take a small downy feather, one of her found objects of the day. This was very touching, considering the associations with Hermes and his winged helmet in the sculpture. This was a further symbolic moment bringing spirit and matter into relationship.[149]

We then took a walk along the riverbank up to the main station. Nighttime was settling in, and a prominent Moon decked the sky above one of the cathedrals. I couldn't resist, so I asked for a group photograph, with the exquisite city lights and buildings adding to this enchanting backdrop.

The morning of our final day, we visited the cemetery in Kusnacht. Near the entrance is a beautiful pond with a number of colourful lotus flowers in bloom, and a sculpture of a couple of herons perched at its edge. After paying our respects in the cemetery, we then progressed to the C. G. Jung House Museum, a few minutes away.[150] My previous visit to the house, some years prior, was restricted to an afternoon with Andreas in Jung's library study and consulting space. The visit now was more spacious, as the house was converted into a museum with tours including access to the back garden.

A couple of impressions from inside the house stood out to me. The first was in the initial meeting room: a large stand-alone heating stove about eight feet in height, and perhaps three or four feet in diameter. In expected Jungian fashion, this portrayed a range of esoteric imagery, such as astrological and alchemical glyphs. At the top was a bird, perhaps a phoenix or pelican. Our tour guide fielded our questions well, explaining its use; especially during the war with fuel shortages and restrictions.

The next room was a fairly large open-space dining room and living room. A new insight was the placing of two pictures, one next to each door that led onto the main house.

---

[149] Of further interest is that Margaret was originally in the photograph I took of the Hermes-tortoise sculpture in the Kunsthaus, though I chose to crop her out of the picture I shared.

[150] My found object of the day was a feather in the pathway, walking up to the front door.

Facing in this direction, the picture on the right was of Galileo, and the one on the left was of David and Goliath. My interpretation is that Jung saw his life myth coinciding with a pivotal moment in history, helping to catalyse a paradigm shift in the Western worldview.

After the house tour, we spent some time in the back garden. Being another hot day, some of us refreshed by wading a bit in the lake.[151] At the other end of the garden was the sculpture of Atmavictu, near the garden room.

Before leaving the house, our MA students had arranged a small ceremony in front of the house, where Patrick presented me (and Lyn, *in abstentia*) with a plaque *Vocatus atque non vocatus deus aderit* ("called or not called, the god will be there"). It was a touching moment and most apt gift, especially being at the front of Jung's house, above which the inscription is placed. After this, our next stop was for lunch, a few minutes' walk along the lake. On the way, we passed the C.G. Jung Institute (and the house of Tina Turner, who died earlier that year).

After a long, lazy lunch, we took a boat trip back into Zurich, having also dispersed somewhat as a group. In Zurich, I was part of a little split-off cluster that trailed through the cathedral with the Chagall windows, a random art gallery visit just outside the cathedral, featuring the work of a Mr. Brainwash.[152] After a short perusal in the Art Brut gallery nearby, we then settled into the smallish Musée Visionnaire. A centrepiece work titled *Späte Insel* (Late Island) caught our eye. The work, by artist Margrit Schlumpf-Portmann (1931-2017), is made in an embroidered "cord painting" style. Its short description in German translates to, "The time

---

[151] As I entered the lake, I noticed a small (recently deceased) fish at my feet. Astonished, considering fish symbolism and Jung, this encounter struck me as quite significant. The previous Age of Pisces now "dead in the water" in the vessel (lake) of the Aquarian *Anthropos*. I sensed that my Italian student Carmen understood, and so was happy she was right there next to me, to share the moment. I took a photo of her foot next to the fish, at the lake edge.

[152] This was Patrick's idea, which paid off as he loved the art style, and was especially smitten to find a Batman (or, rather, a parody as Fatman) sculpture.

in nature, death, and resurrection. The first pulsation in my garden after severe lonely winter."

This struck me for some reason. About a hundred and ten years earlier, 1913, was the beginning of the return of Jung's soul. In his *Liber Novus*, we read: "My soul, where are you? Do you hear me? I speak, I call you — are you there? I have shaken the dust of all the lands from my feet, and I have come to you, I am with you. After long years of wandering, I have come to you again." [153] It felt as if something similar, albeit on a much less grandiose scale, was occurring with me. This was the year of having accomplished a few modest life goals, yet much of this came at the expense of my own soul care.

Over the past twenty years or so, I had been running a part-time course on top of my full-time lecturing load. Amidst all of this and bringing up a family, I had also done a PhD, shape-shifted careers from technology and sustainable energy into the arts, and had recently been key to pioneering the MA programme. Much of my professional work was also quite cognitive — more of an *oratorium* than a *laboratorium*, to use an alchemical metaphor. This left precious little time to nurture my own psyche. Our Zurich trip and the prospect of summer recess began to feel like a return of my soul. The symbol of the flower, from the beginning of our trip, was perhaps also a prospective of this fresh, vital development.

"The first pulsation in my garden after severe lonely winter," Freudian interpretations aside, might be read as a symbol in a "Big Dream" sense. In a word, the Jungian approach could be summarised as "soul." His psychology is very much a counterpoint to the disenchantment of the World, Eliot's Wasteland, and a pervasive loss of soul that has gained momentum in our times. Jung's life and works are, for many, a healing counterpoint.

[153] C.G. Jung, *The Red Book: Liber Novus*, ed. Sonu Shamdasani, trans. John Peck, Mark Kyburz, and Sonu Shamdasani (New York, NY: W.W. Norton, 2009), 232.

EPILOGUE

Our first contact days in our Master's of Arts program are typically on the mythic imagination. Here we ask the question, "What is your personal myth?" This was a question Jung famously asked himself after suffering the crisis of his religious upbringing and then a falling-out with Freud and psychoanalysis. In answering this question, he voluntarily fell down the rabbit hole into the unconscious, into deeper strata of the psyche than what psychoanalysis had to offer.

He would term this a "confrontation with the unconscious," in which he animatedly engaged with imaginal figures. These were recorded in a number of journals known as the Black Books. Over the next few years, this inspired much of his so-called *Red Book*, or *Liber Novus* ("New Book"), created in the style of an illuminated manuscript with calligraphic script and impressive artwork. These experiences became the formative material, his *prima materia*, for a lifetime of work. It was the volcanic lava out of which his psychology — analytical psychology — would be fashioned, an alchemical Opus that transmuted a wound into a work. Recognising its great value, he would encourage his patients to embark on a similar journey, and to record their experiences in a "holy book," a "cathedral of the soul."

These experiences would also form the basis for the discovery of his own personal life myth. Our culture that has largely devalued the soul sees little point or purpose in spending time with the manifestations of psyche, be they dreams, active imaginations, synchronistic phenomena, bodily symptoms, or raw creative expression. In alchemy, this is expressed in symbolic form as the dung heap, or as menses, faeces, or urine, something of lowly value, even despised. Yet it is within this, as a symbol, where the treasure is to be found.

In Jungian psychology, this is the initial stage of an analysis: shadow work. An inglorious task, it is a labour that finds expression in images such as washing dirty laundry. In this work, though, there can be inklings of a numinous core. With the key of amplifying knowledge, we more easily have the possibility of recognising mythopoetic threads. If we engage creatively with this, we have the opportunity of transmuting a wound into a work.

Furthermore, our wound can be inextricably related to a cultural wound. It might touch on the Grail legend question posed to the Fisher King: "What ails thee?" The twentieth century saw two World Wars, a "disenchantment of the world" (Weber), The Wasteland (Eliot), and philosophical emanations such as the birth of Absurdism (Camus) and Existential Nihilism (Kierkegaard). In a nutshell, we are suffering a malaise, a soul loss. For Jung, we have lost our holding myth. To quote: "One without a myth ... is like one uprooted, having no true link either with the past, or with the ancestral life which continues within him, or yet with contemporary human society."[154]

His discovery and immersive engagement with alchemy during the last three decades of his life addressed such concerns. In the documentary film *A Matter of Heart*, his collaborator and *Soror Mystica* Marie-Louise von Franz distils this essence: "I think that the Christian myth, on which we have lived, has degenerated and become one-sided and insufficient. I think alchemy is the complete myth ... [it is] a richer completion and continuation of the Christian myth." Continuing, she states that "alchemy: confronts the problem of the opposites; of the feminine; and of matter."

She optimistically touches on the topic of opposites in terms of the enlightenment: "the rationalism of the seventeenth century ... had one advantage after all: it drove father-spirit and mother-matter so far apart that now we can reunite them in a cleaner way."[155] This gives a sense of a big idea in

---

[154] C. G. Jung, *Symbols of Transformation*, trans. R. F. C. Hull, ed. Herbert Read, Michael Fordham, and Gerhard Adler, *The Collected Works of C. G. Jung*, vol. 5 (London: Routledge & Kegan Paul, 1956), xxiv.

[155] Marie-Louise von Franz, *Psyche and Matter* (Boston: Shambhala, 1988), 157.

Jung's alchemical worldview, the alchemical *coniunctio,* its relevance for the myth for our times, and of dreaming the myth onward.

As I elaborated in my Mercurius book, Jung was also embroiled in the notion of a transition of the Ages and believed we were in a changing myth: from The Age of Pisces, the Fishes, to the Age of Aquarius, the Water Bearer. In essence, a shift from *separatio* symbolism to *coniunctio* symbolism. If a key symbol of the Piscean Age is the sword (a cross), then a key symbol of the Aquarian Age is a vessel, or *vas.*

Jung's milieu was also part of a great syncretism — the coming together in a large cultural melting pot of the world's wisdom traditions. His writings, for instance, include commentaries on texts entering the Western cultural imagination, such as the *I Ching, The Secret of the Golden Flower*, and the *Tibetan Book of the Dead.*

After his death in 1961, space exploration allowed for a view of the Earth for the first time. Notably, the Moon landing in 1969, and then a more distant view (from Saturn) in 1998, where the Earth was described as a "pale blue dot." It is possible that our task, in the 21st century, includes the re-assembly of a "Humpty Dumpty" that has had a great fall. Our myth is shattered. Perhaps it will take some centuries to forge a new "one earth" myth as Murray Stein and others have alluded to, as a myth that can satisfyingly contain the complex nature of *Anthropos* in the world and cosmos. Or maybe we should embrace, as Hillman and some post-Jungians would have, an intrinsic pluralism.

❦

Reflecting on this project, I realise how my worldview and experiences, as recorded in a series of journals over the years, mirror a shattered myth. I believe this is not unique to me, but symptomatic of our times. Yet within the detritus of these broken images, there are glimmerings of something hopeful and of great value. It feels as if I have been divining, as a dowser might, a central mythic figure as the *Anima Mundi.* There are intimations of a re-connection with such a figure that communicates in an enigmatic symbolic language. If this is so, then a valuation of the "dungheap" of our dreams, reveries, synchronicities, symptoms, and creative expressions might contain the gold that, through an Opus, might be wrought into a work: a rediscovery and a celebration of our place in the world and cosmos, and one that re-members our relationship to a beloved.

About the Author

Mathew Mather is a lecturer, writer and researcher in the Department of Fine Art and Education at Limerick School of Art and Design, Technological University of the Shannon, in Ireland. He is author of *The Alchemical Mercurius: Esoteric Symbol of Jung's Life and Works*, based on a PhD on Jung and alchemy, and has also authored a number of book chapters and articles. He is director of the *MA in Art, Psyche and the Creative Imagination* and the *Certificate in Jungian Psychology with Art Therapy*. His professional interests include the intersection of depth psychology with the arts, Jung's mature work (with emphasis on alchemy and synchronicity), as well as his Black Books and Red Book or *Liber Novus*.

In his spare time Mathew enjoys family, reading, nature, the arts, environment, Tai Chi, cooking, and friends. He has two lovely daughters Katie and Karla, and lives with his wife Lyn and cat Munks, next to the Shannon river in Limerick. This current work is a first attempt in the style of a non-fiction magical journey, and as a form of memoir.

About Sul Books

Born from a collaboration of two long-time independent esoteric publishers, and named to honor the Suleviae — the sisterhood of goddesses revered at springs throughout Europe — Sul Books is dedicated to publishing works that manifest aspects of the sacred sight that heals what humans have harmed.

BIBLIOGRAPHY

Alexander, Eben. *Proof of Heaven: A Neurosurgeon's Journey into the Afterlife*. New York: Simon & Schuster, 2012.

Attar, Farīd ud-Dīn. *The Conference of the Birds*. Translated by Sholeh Wolpé. New York: W. W. Norton & Company, 2017.

Aziz, Robert. *C. G. Jung's Psychology of Religion and Synchronicity*. Albany: State University of New York Press, 1990.

Bair, Deirdre. *Jung: A Biography*. Boston: Little, Brown and Company, 2003.

Begg, Deike. *Synchronicity: The Promise of Coincidence*. London: HarperCollins Publishers, 2001.

Brooks, Michael. *The Quantum Astrologer's Handbook: A History of the Renaissance Mathematics That Birthed Imaginary Numbers, Probability, and the New Physics of the Universe*. London: Scribe Publications, 2017.

Chatwyn, Bruce. *Utz*. London: Picador, 1989.

CNN Business. "Elon Musk Warns AI Could Cause 'Civilization Destruction' Even as He Invests in It." April 18, 2023. Accessed October 2, 2025.

Condren, Mary. *The Serpent and the Goddess: Women, Religion, and Power in Celtic Ireland*. San Francisco: Harper & Row, 1989.

Corbin, Henry. *Jung, Buddhism, and the Incarnation of Sophia: Unpublished Writings from the Philosopher of the Soul*. Rochester, VT: Inner Traditions, 2019.

DiPippo, Gregory. "Symbols of the Four Evangelists." *New Liturgical Movement*. October 23, 2018. https://www.newliturgicalmovement.org/2018/10/symbols-of-four-evangelists.html.

Doolan, Maureen. "Pari, David Bohm and a Scarab Beetle." *Pari Perspectives*, no. 5 (2020).

Dunlea, Marian. *BodyDreaming in the Treatment of Developmental Trauma: An Embodied Therapeutic Approach*. London: Routledge, 2019.

Earth Version 2 Pty Ltd. *Earth 2®*. Launched November 2020. Accessed October 2, 2025. https://earth2.io/.

Eliade, Mircea. *Shamanism: Archaic Techniques of Ecstasy*. Translated by Willard R. Trask. Bollingen Series 76. Princeton, NJ: Princeton University Press, 2004.

Fellows, Andrew. *Gaia, Psyche and Deep Ecology: Navigating Climate Change in the Anthropocene*. London: Routledge, 2019.

Fraleigh, Sondra. *Butoh: Metamorphic Dance and Global Alchemy*. Urbana: University of Illinois Press, 2010.

Fulcanelli. *Fulcanelli: Master Alchemist: Le Mystère des Cathédrales: Esoteric Interpretation of the Hermetic Symbols of the Great Work*. Translated from the French by Mary Sworder. Albuquerque, NM: Brotherhood of Life, 1984.

"Gimme Shelter: COVID-19 Pandemic — Reflections and Strategies for our Current World Transits 4-16-20." By Rick Tarnas, Laura Michetti, Lilly Falconer, and Chad Harris. YouTube video, 1:56:07. Posted April 17, 2020. https://www.youtube.com/watch?v=YR-keIe5p_A.

Goodchild, Veronica. *Songlines of the Soul: Pathways to a New Vision for a New Century*. Boston: Nicolas-Hays Inc, 2012.

Haas, Jack. *In, and Of: Memoirs of a Mystic Journey Along Canada's Wild West Coast*. Vancouver, BC: Iconoclast Press, 2002.

Hederman, Mark Patrick. *Tarot, Talisman or Taboo?: Reading the World as Symbol*. Blackrock, Co. Dublin, Ireland: Currach Press, 2003.

Hillman, James. *Animal Presences: Uniform Edition of the Writings of James Hillman, Vol. 9*. Uniform Edition of the Writings of James Hillman. Putnam, CT: Spring Publications, 2008.

Jung, C. G. *Aion: Researches into the Phenomenology of the Self*. Translated by R. F. C. Hull. The Collected Works of C. G. Jung, vol. 9, pt. 2. London: Routledge & Kegan Paul, 1981.

———. *Alchemical Studies*. Translated by R.F.C. Hull. Vol. 13 of The Collected Works of C.G. Jung. London: Routledge & Kegan Paul, 1981.

———. "The Integration of the Personality." In *The Symbolic Life*, translated by R. F. C. Hull. Edited by Herbert Read, Michael Fordham, and Gerhard Adler. The Collected Works of C. G. Jung, vol. 18. London: Routledge & Kegan Paul, 1981.

———. *Mysterium Coniunctionis: An Inquiry into the Separation and Synthesis of Psychic Opposites in Alchemy*. Translated by R.F.C. Hull. Vol. 14 of The Collected Works of C.G. Jung. London: Routledge & Kegan Paul, 1981.

———. "Psychological Commentary on 'The Tibetan Book of the Great Liberation.'" In *The Structure and Dynamics of the Psyche*, translated by R.F.C. Hull, 2nd ed., 407–39. Vol. 8 of The Collected Works of C.G. Jung. London: Routledge & Kegan Paul, 1981.

———. "The Psychology of the Transference." In *The Collected Works of C. G. Jung, Volume 16: The Practice of Psychotherapy*, translated by R. F. C. Hull. London: Routledge, 1981.

———. "The Spirit Mercurius." In *Alchemical Studies*, translated by R.F.C. Hull, 191–254. Vol. 13 of The Collected Works of C.G. Jung. London: Routledge & Kegan Paul, 1981.

———. *The Structure and Dynamics of the Psyche*. Translated by R.F.C. Hull. 2nd ed. Vol. 8 of The Collected Works of C.G. Jung. London: Routledge & Kegan Paul, 1981.

———. *Symbols of Transformation*. Translated by R. F. C. Hull. Edited by Herbert Read, Michael Fordham, and Gerhard Adler. The Collected Works of C. G. Jung, vol. 5. London: Routledge & Kegan Paul, 1981.

Jung, C. G. *Memories, Dreams, Reflections*. Recorded and edited by Aniela Jaffé. Translated by Richard Winston and Clara Winston. New York: Vintage Books, 1989.

Jung, C. G. *Visions: Notes on the Seminar Given in 1930–1934*. Edited by Claire Douglas. London: Routledge, 1998.

Jung, C. G. *The Red Book: Liber Novus*. Edited by Sonu Shamdasani. Translated by John Peck, Mark Kyburz, and Sonu Shamdasani. New York, NY: W. W. Norton, 2009.

Lenihan, Eddie. *Meeting the Other Crowd: The Fairy Stories of Hidden Ireland*. Dublin: Gill & Macmillan, 2003.

Mag Fhloinn, Billy. *Website of Billy Mag Fhloinn*. Accessed October 2, 2025. http://www.tradition.ie/.

Main, Roderick. *The Rupture of Time: Synchronicity and Jung's Critique of Modern Western Culture*. New York: Routledge, 2004.

Main, Roderick. *Revelations of Chance: Synchronicity as Spiritual Experience*. SUNY series in Transpersonal and Humanistic Psychology. Albany, NY: State University of New York Press, 2007.

Mather, Mathew. *The Alchemical Mercurius: Esoteric Symbol of Jung's Life and Works*. London: Routledge, 2014.

Mather, Mathew. "Jung's Red Book and the Alchemical Coniunctio." In *Jung's Red Book for Our Time: Searching for Soul under Postmodern Conditions, Volume 3*, edited by Murray Stein and Thomas Arzt. Asheville, NC: Chiron Publications, 2019.

Mather, Mathew. "A Green-Gold Scarab Symbol for the Turning of an Age?" *International Journal of Jungian Studies* 16, no. 1 (2024): 3–18.

Miller, Arthur I. *137: Jung, Pauli, and the Pursuit of a Scientific Obsession*. New York: W. W. Norton & Company, 2010.

Moran, Sean. "Smooching by the Seine." *Philosophy Now*, no. 148 (February/March 2022): 60.

National Geographic. "King Cobra Reticulated Python Fight." February 5, 2018. https://www.nationalgeographic.com/animals/article/king-cobra-reticulated-python-fight-battle-photo-spd.

Nichols, Sallie. *Jung and Tarot: An Archetypal Journey*. New York: Weiser Books, 1998.

Ronnberg, Ami, and Kathleen Martin, eds. *The Book of Symbols: Reflections on Archetypal Images*. Cologne: Taschen; New York: Archive for Research in Archetypal Symbolism, 2010.

Sagan, Carl. *Pale Blue Dot: A Vision of the Human Future in Space*. New York: Random House, 1994.

Sage, Amanda. *Amanda Sage Art*. Accessed October 2, 2025. https://www.amandasage.com/.

Saner, Emine. "The Hateful Eighth: Artists at the Frontline of Ireland's Abortion Rights Battle." *The Guardian*, April 12, 2018. https://www.theguardian.com/artanddesign/2018/apr/12/the-hateful-eighth-artists-frontline-ireland-abortion-rights-battle-eighth-amendment.

Stein, Murray. "A World Shadow: COVID 19." Interview by Robert S. Henderson. Chiron Publications, March 2020. https://chironpublications.com/a-world-shadow-covid-19/.

Schweizer, Andreas. *The Sun God's Journey through the Netherworld: Reading the Ancient Egyptian Amduat.* Edited by David Lorton. Ithaca, NY: Cornell University Press, 2010.

Tarnas, Richard. *Cosmos and Psyche: Intimations of a New World View.* New York: Plume, 2007.

Teikemeier, Lothar. *Tarot Wheel.* Accessed October 2, 2025. http://www.tarot-wheel.net.

The Pari Center. Accessed October 2, 2025. https://paricenter.com/.

Thunberg, Greta. *No One Is Too Small to Make a Difference.* New York: Penguin Books, 2019.

Todorova, Rotislava. "The Migrating Symbol: Vesica Piscis from the Pythagoreans to Christianity." *Vesalius* 20, no. 1 (2014): 4–12.

Von Franz, Marie-Louise. *Shadow and Evil in Fairytales.* Dallas, TX: Spring Publications, 1974.

Von Franz, Marie-Louise. *On Divination and Synchronicity: The Psychology of Meaningful Chance.* Toronto: Inner City Books, 1980.

Von Franz, Marie-Louise. *Psyche and Matter.* Boston: Shambhala, 1988.

Wildermuth, Rhyd. *A People's Guide to Tarot: A Primer for Everyone.* Ritona, 2024.

Wilhelm, Richard, trans. *The Secret of the Golden Flower: A Chinese Book of Life.* With a European Commentary by C. G. Jung. Translated into English by Cary F. Baynes. Revised ed. London: Routledge and Kegan Paul, 1981.

INDEX